Thomas Jordan's Diary

A. Scott Earle, Editor

ISBN 978-0-6151-6013-9

Larkspur Books. 2440 N. Bogus Basin Rd., Boise, Idaho 83702.
Tel.: 208-344-0079
web site: www.larkspurbooks.com
email: larkspur1@cableone.net

Created, designed and published in the United States

First edition

For Thomas Jordan's descendents

Thomas Jordan's Notebook

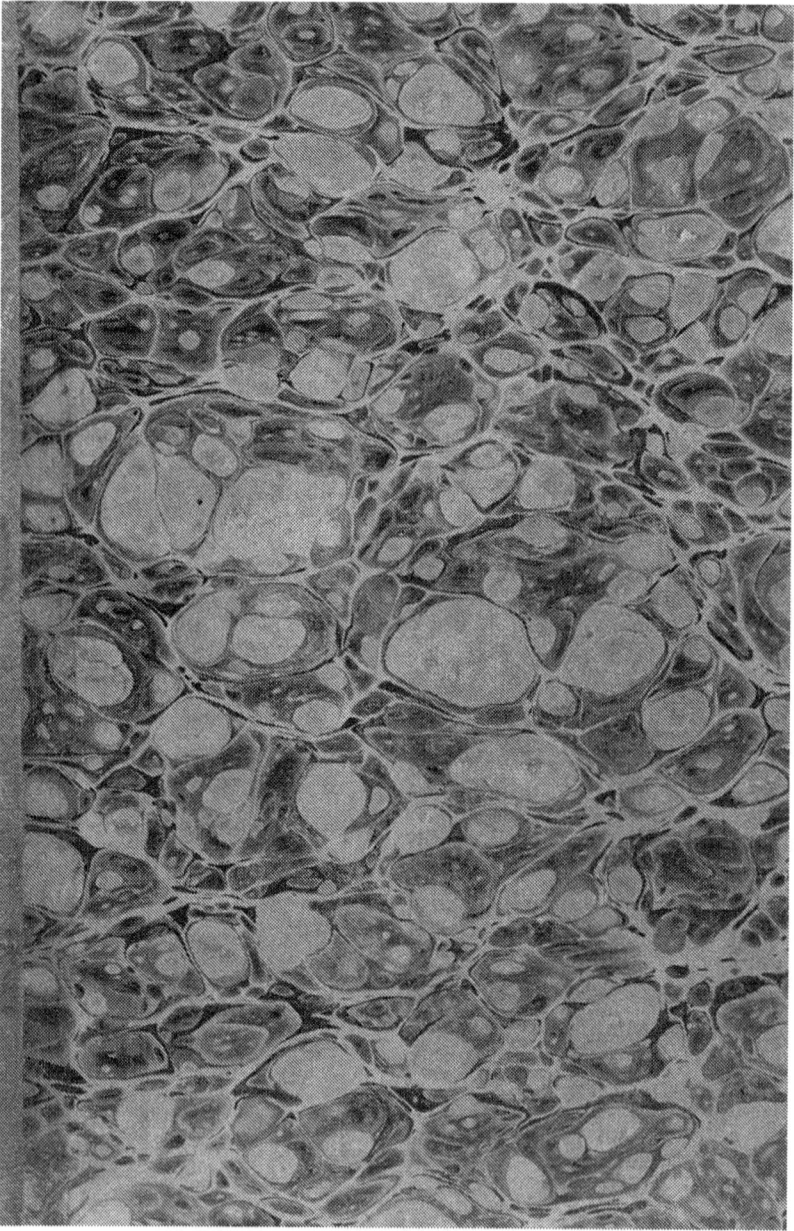

Bought of Gore & Holbrook at Freeport February 20th 1845

Thomas Jordan's Diary
1845-1849

When I was a child in the 1930s, we drove from our home in Lexington, Massachusetts, several times a year to visit two great-aunts in Lewiston, Maine. The drive was long. No interstate highways then, only narrow two lane blacktop roads replete with "thank-you-marms"—sudden dips that caused one's stomach to rise as the body passed briefly through zero-gravity. Lewiston is separated from its twin city, Auburn, by the Androscoggin River. The river plunges over falls a short distance above the bridge between the two cities—a spectacular sight for a child, and enough in itself to make our visits memorable. The aunts, Mattie and Bertha Hinkley, sisters of my paternal grandmother, lived on the second floor of an ungainly gray clapboard duplex. The house had no central heating. A coal burning stove, stately, tall, black and pot-bellied, stood in the living room. It, and a range in the kitchen, kept the two rooms warm, but the rest of the house remained cold—often *very* cold, during the long Maine winters—as I learned during several overnight visits to Lewiston.

The aunts often spoke of their grandfather, Thomas Jordan. He had been, they said, a sea captain. There is little in his journal, however, to suggest that their grandfather spent much time at sea, although he was in his forties when he wrote it, so he may well have gone to sea as a young man. Over the years several Jordan artifacts came into my possession. His maple bed became mine when I turned five. TJ had made the scrolled headboard from a single board almost three feet wide. Massive square beams connect sturdy, turned bedposts. He perforated the beams at intervals for the rope webbing used then to support a mattress. At some point the ropes had been replaced with an innerspring and a squeaky horsehair mattress. The bed was so high that I could barely climb onto it. A brass, maple-handled bed-warmer came later. Its worn and blackened pan showed that it was used often in cold weather. A plain, finely crafted maple bureau, with drawers made of neatly dove-tailed maple and lined with white pine, completed the bedroom set. And then there was his diary.

The Diary: My great aunts passed away after the second World War, and Thomas Jordan's diary came to me as part of their legacy. It covered a period of four years and four months, from February of 1845 to June of 1849. TJ lived in Webster, Maine. A note on the front free endpage of the diary states that he had bought the book from Gore and Holbrook in Freeport on February 20, 1845. Seemingly, it was meant to be a ledger. The book was well made and only now, more than a century and a half later, have its pages loosened with the stress of electronic scanning. The boards are covered with hand-marbled paper; the spine is bound in leather. Each page is seven and a half inches high and six inches wide. The pages are lined throughout. The horizontal lines are barely visible now although vertical red lines, common to ledgers, remain as evidence of the book's original purpose. The pages are a bit age-yellowed, but they are also intact throughout. Clearly the paper was good quality rag rather than the acidic wood pulp stock commonly used in mid-nineteenth century books—paper that disintegrates today at a touch.

I browsed through TJ's diary from time to time and found that it provided a vivid picture of life in rural Maine more than a century and a half ago. From the first, I thought that the diary should be transcribed, a job that necessarily had to be put off until I retired and could give it the time that it deserved. TJ's flowing, compulsively neat, cursive script is beginning to fade although it is still quite legible. When I transcribed it, trying to decipher words here and there, I saw TJ in my mind's eye, writing his brief entries each evening by the light of a candle or whale-oil lamp. He hardly seems to have had posterity in mind, rather he simply noted, briefly, each day's highlights, ending with a remark on the weather.

I have no way of knowing whether TJ kept other diaries before and after mine, but my volume seems too well organized to be a onetime endeavor. There must have been others, but if they still exist I have no idea where they might be. No matter, my single volume tells us much about life in rural New England in the first half of the 19th century. A son is born, Thomas's sister and his father die. Many other deaths are recorded, mostly without further comment. Barns are raised, crops are planted and harvested. Hired men come and go, animals are slaughtered, and produce is sold. He notes accidents, injuries and other unusual events: John Quincy Adams dies, the railroad comes to Lewiston. He and his family celebrate some holidays and ignore others. It is all recorded in his neat hand; TJ's diary is truly a window to the past.

My forebear was no Samuel Pepys. The literary value of what he wrote is nil. His terse journal entries tend to be dull and repetitive; clearly he was writing for himself. He plants in the spring: beans, peas, wheat, corn and greens, and he harvests in late summer and autumn. He takes farm produce to market, carefully noting how much he receives in dollars, shillings, and pennies. He notes his daily activities and day to day events as they occur in his neighborhood. Nevertheless—despite the leanness of his entries—there is wealth in what he wrote. It takes only a little imagination, on sampling his diary, for us to visualize what farm life was like in Maine, a century and a half ago. We can not help but wish that TJ had been a bit more detailed about his day-to-day life. What was the inside of his house like; what were the living arrangements? He purchased books, but did not note their titles. What did Mary Ann cook and bake? How often did they bathe? How were the children schooled? As a physician, I often reflected on the family's health. What caused TJ's severe "diziness" and Mary Ann's "cholic." Why did he take his fourteen year old daughter to see "the famous Dr. Mann?" What exactly were the medicines that Dr. Garcelon provided? What was the "gum" that Dr. Mudget gave to Sally for her cancer? TJ mentions two amputations in the journal in 1848. Was ether anesthesia, introduced two years earlier, used for the surgery?

Thomas had a large farm and much needed to be done. He had to care for livestock—pigs, sheep, and cattle—and break oxen to the yoke. He had to construct and repair buildings and maintain fences. He built a "portch" for the house and, with much work and a lot of blasting powder, he dug a well. He hayed, slaughtered, sheared, plowed, harrowed, lumbered, hauled, gathered wood for the winter and in between made shoes for his family and for his neighbors. He often made things for others: oxen yokes, sleds, sleighs, wagons, and wheels. He was active in the community's activities, attending Sunday services regularly. TJ makes frequent mention of neighbors, especially the Dyers, the Carvills and other Jordans whose sons worked for him as hired hands, by the day, week, or month. His family sometimes turned out to help in the fields. Although TJ experienced both injury and illness during the time covered in his journal, he almost always carried on, only rarely missing a day or two of work. Nowhere in his journal is there a hint of complaint; Thomas Jordan's life, it seems, was fulfilled and secure.

Such a strenuous life, presumably without tobacco or alcohol, made for healthy longevity. Still, diseases were prevalent and I suspect that most of the neighbors' children who died suddenly did so from infection of one type or another. He mentions smallpox, for example, several times. Nevertheless, his family—other than his sister Sally who dies of cancer—were healthy and long lived. TJ's father died at 83, and TJ lived to be

86. Women, sadly, were less fortunate, a reflection of the perils of child-birth in the pre-antiseptic era.

The Transcription: I tried to be meticulous in transcribing the entries, and to present the diary as my ancestor wrote it. A few, and only a few, alterations were necessary. First, because TJ did not start a new line for each day, and because all of his entries run together, I began each day's entry on a new line. Next, his words are sometimes illegible, or are clearly missing. I have indicated these lapses with brackets, including a best guess when warranted, and a question mark [?] when the meaning is completely obscure. TJ's punctuation and spelling are inconsistent; he used apostrophes, commas and periods erratically and usually did not indicate separate clauses, particularly when writing about the weather. The result can be off-putting; clearly "...dull Mary Ann..." meant that the day, not his wife, was dull. In such instances I have added a comma or period. These emendations are infrequent, and they do ease the flow—otherwise the punctuation is as TJ entered it.

I have also retained his spelling. Some words are clearly misspelled, others were spelled correctly for the time. English has changed since TJ penned his diary. The words "waggon" and "portch" were spelled that way in his day. He also, correctly, "wed in the garden"—the past particle of the verb "weed" then was "wed," just as the past participle of "bleed" and "feed" are "bled" and "fed" today. Other words that we use now had different meanings then. "Garden sauce" meant garden vegetables, greens especially, and "pink-eye" was a kind of potato. Some of his words are now obsolete; for example "pung" for a sled, "bunks" for fence posts, and many others as well. The Appalachians are said to have been a repository of old English, but so too was Thomas Jordan's Maine. The Oxford English Dictionary (OED) has proved invaluable; many of the obscure words in his diary are characterized in the dictionary as *arch.* or *obs.*, and some of the citations for these go back many centuries. Finally, mistakes in transcripion inevitably occur. I have tried to find and correct them all, but a few undoubtedly persist.*

Genealogy: The name Jordan is an old one that apparently originated with crusaders and others who visited the Holy Land and returned bearing water from—and may have been baptised in—the River Jordan. It is a common name in parts of England. The first of Thomas Jordan's forebears, Robert Jordan, came to the New World in 1639, probably from

---

*An electronic scan of TJ's diary on CD is available for any who wish to consult the original: see page 155.

Dorsetshire or Devonshire. He is known to have been living on Richmond Island, near today's Portland, Maine, in 1641. He was a minister and an upstanding person, although he was also thoroughly disliked by New England Puritans and was twice jailed for performing marriage ceremonies and baptisms according to the rites of the Church of England.

Robert Jordan's oldest son, Dominicus, was born prior to 1634. He too had six children by two marriages before being tomahawked by "friendly" Indians in 1705. Dominicus's youngest son, Nathaniel (1696-1783), was taken by Indians to Canada; he was eventually freed in 1713. Nathaniel married twice and a son by his first marriage—also named Nathaniel (1733-1783)—had nine children. Our Thomas Jordan's father, Ephraim (1764-1846), was this Nathaniel's second son.

Ephraim Jordan was born at Cape Elizabeth, Maine, where the family had lived for three generations. He was an industrious man who learned that there was good land close to the Androscoggin River in what later became Webster, Maine. Ephraim purchased 105 acres of heavily timbered land in 1788, built a log cabin, and married his second cousin, Ann Jordan (d.1829) in 1791. Ephraim's brother, Abner, also purchased land nearby a few years later. Abner's family is frequently mentioned in TJ's diary, as are other Jordans who settled in the area.

Our Thomas Jordan (1801-1886), was Ephraim and Ann Jordan's fourth child. TJ married Mary Ann Hinkley in 1831, and they had seven children. All are mentioned in his diary. Ann was the oldest (1832-1901), followed by Elizabeth (1833-1861), Rowena (1835-1918), Melissa (1836-1917), and Martha (1839-1880). Holman (or Holmon, 1844-?) was their first son. A second son—and their youngest child—Albert (1847-1893), was born during the diary years.

TJ's and Mary Ann's second child, Elizabeth, married a distant cousin, Andrew Hinkley (1809-1902), in 1857. Elizabeth died four years later. Andrew then married her sister Martha in 1862. (Andrew knew a good thing, for in his old age he married Ann, yet another of the Jordan girls, in 1892; she was then sixty years old.) Andrew Hinkley and Martha Jordan had three daughters, including the two maiden great-aunts mentioned above, and my paternal grandmother Essie Jordan Hinkley (1867-1927). Essie married Eugene Vinton Earle (1866-1924) of Lisbon, Maine, in 1891. I am the oldest son (1924-) of their third child, Arthur Hinkley Earle (1896-1962).

A. Scott Earle
Boise, Idaho
September, 2007

N. Webster, February. Monday 17th 1845
Clear & very pleasant sun, the sleet began to fall
from the trees quite early with a tremendous
crash, I went into the woods & cut some stuff for
timber & one load of wood & went up to Jacob
Whitney who was cutting ship timber on Mr
Robinson's land to sell him a stick or tree that he
wanted, Afternoon I hauled out the timber & wood
I cut in forenoon, warm & the snow quite soft
—18th We went up to Wentworth Jordans on a
visit, Jacob Gould & wife here, very warm again
—19th I put out hams to smoke, enlarged a stall
in the stable &c, quite thawy,—20th I went to N.
Yarmouth & got ten bushels plaster, froze last
night & fine sleighing, dull and a prospect of rain
some thawy,—21st Still dull, Mr Pettengill
& wife Mr A. Lewis & wife here I attended to no
business—22d We went down to John Goulds
on a visit very remarkable warm & pleasant day
water ran merrily, no frost last night—Sun. 23d
We went up to Mr Ayers to see Miss Dyer, she rather
comfortable to day but quite feeble, dull in forenoon
quite rainy in afternoon, Seward Sham let a load here
at night

Webster February Monday 17th 1845

Clear & very pleasant sun, the sleet began to fall from the trees quite early with a tremenduous crash. I went into the woods & cut some stuff[1] for timber & one load of wood & went up to Jacob Whitney who was cutting ship timber on Mr. Robinson's land to sell him a stick or tree that he wanted. Afternoon I hauld out the timber & wood I cut in forenoon, warm & the snow quite soft.[2]

—18th We went up to Wentworth Jordans on a visit, Jacob Gould & wife here, very warm again.

—19th I put our hams to smoke, & enlarged a stall in the stable &c. quite thawy

—20th I Went to N. Yarmouth & got ten bushels plaster[3], froze last night & fine sleighing, dull and a prospect of rain some thawy.

—21st Still dull. Mr Pettengill & wife , Mr A. Davis & wife here. I attended to no business

—22d. We went down to John Goulds on a visit, very remarkable warm & pleasant day, water run merrily, no frost last night

—Sun. 23d We went up to Mr. Dyers to see Miss Dyer, she's rather comfortable today, but quite feeble, dull in forenoon quite rainy in afternoon, Seward Ham let a load here at night.

---

1. TJ purchased the book that he used for his journal on the 20th of February. This entry, for the 17th, was pre-dated by three days.

2. TJ often uses the word "stuff," to refer to timber out of which something will be built or crafted. His usage is closer to the word's original meaning—that of material, stores or provisions—than to its present day usage as a catch-all term for almost anything. "Wood," on the other hand, was used to designate fuel.

1 TJ used the plaster (lime) on his fields. See note, page 87, August 12, 1847

Webster February Monday 24th 1845

I help'd E. Jordan 2d hew[1] fencing posts very pleasant & quite thawy

—25th I bought one bushel of herdsgrass seed[2] of Seward Ham at 2.25 per bush. I went up and got Mrs. Wentworth to stay with Sally she being quite [sick] last night while we went to the Bend to carry bacon &c. very pleasant the snow runs finely.

—26th I went over to James Crowleys to see a pair of steers[3] of William's he wishing to trade them for my oxen, so awful homley I would not have them, E. Jordan 2d help'd me saw up logs for the mill, pleasant & thawy.

—27 I help'd N. Jordan on a stump machine[4] Niah Hinkley chop'd wood at the door for me & I help'd N. Jordan again. My cousin John Jordan from Cape Elisabeth here.

—March 1st I and Niah H. chopd wood at the door

—Sunday 2d Reuben [&?] Drusilla Dyer with the little babe down here, sister Dyer is some better

—3rd & 4th I was at work for N. Jordan again.

—5th A smart snow storm in fore—noon, help'd N. Jordan raise his machine, some rain in afternoon

—6th Clear & very high wind from N.W. I was down to the mill & got signers to a request to the Selectmen for selling the old magazine[5]

---

1 "hew" means either to shape timber, or to cut down timber.

2 herds-grass: A name for various grasses grown for hay or pasture; esp. common timothy, *Phleum pratense*, or a bent (red-top), such as *Agrostis gigantea*, OED. "steers" are castrated bulls that are less than four years old; *i.e.* young oxen in this usage,.

4 The OED says only "*stump-machine*. U.S.. A machine for extracting tree-stumps." Neither this or other listings mention the nature of the machine, *e.g.* whether based on a lever or a pulley system.

5. "Magazine" implies a store-house of some type; it sometimes had the more specialized connotation of storing arms, gun-powder, etc.

Webster February [March] Thursday 6th 1845

I closed[1] a pair of shoes for Mary Ann in afternoon & sold our old oxen to Jeremia Crowley for $62.50 very high wind

—7th I hauld logs to the mill all day I calld in to see the young bride, wife of Capt Jesse Davis, married yesterday, indulged in some pleasantry with them for a few minutes

—8th I hauld logs again & all, dull & moderate, John Jordan & Lavinia Marr started for home yesterday morning Fire at Lewiston, A Barn belonging to _ Pickard

—Sunday 9th Dull Mary Ann was over to Enoch Hinkleys

—10th I broke flax,[2] dull in afternoon

—11th I finishd Mary Ann a pair of shoes & taped[3] some of the childrens

—12th I broke flax again & finishd, we was up to Mr. Robinson's on evening visit

—13th Rather pleasant, I dressed flax

—14th I went into the woods & got two load of wood commenced snowing about noon & continued to fall damp all the afternoon

—15th I got horse shod in forenoon & taped a pair of shoes in afternoon dull & rather cool, nearly a foot of snow fell last night

—16th I and Ann went up to B. Dyers poor sleighing.

---

1 "closed" is a 19th c.. shoemakers term meaning to sew the leather parts of the shoe's upper together.

2 "Broke" as used here means "To comb wool roughly, being the first process in carding." The OED notes that the use of "break" in this context is obsolete or archaic. Two examples are given; both are from Shakespeare.

3 TJ means "tapped," another shoemaker's term. To "tap" shoes means to "add a thickness of leather to the sole or heel." OED. Probably derived from the small wooden pegs that were tapped into place to hold the sole leather.

Webster March Sun. 16th 1845

Mrs. Dyer appears to be somewhat better

—17th I went down to Factoryville and carried some corn in ears to get some cobmeal for cows, went in to their town meeting at town house[1] & round home by way of N Hinkley's & brought Elizabeth home.

—18th We went down to see Mr. R. Ham who is quite unwell

—19th I finishd dressing flax quite pleasant

—20th Cold & squally I went up to Greene to carry home a buck[2] of E. Barrels esq, fair sleighing from home to Greene

—21st Very cold last night, I chopd some wood at the door, cold and windy to day

—22nd More pleasant to day I chopd wood again

—23rd Very pleasant indeed, at home till evening when I went down to Capt. Davis, learnd that Mr. Hussey preachd at four corners to day on an engagement for half of the time for another year

—24th I went to annual town meeting Jesse Davis P. M. Garcelon & Malvin Henderson chosen select men Assessors & Overseers of poor J. B. Jordan Treasurer & Samson Colby Collector moderate & some thawy

—25th Cooler & some windy I chopd wood at the door

—26th & 27th Niah Hinkley helpd me chop wood at the door, all chopd & split some

---

1 TJ often speaks of the "town house" in his journal. The term, in common use at the time, refers to what we would now refer to as a "town hall"

2 TJ is referring to a ram.

Webster March Friday 28th 1845

I split & piled up wood

—29th I went to mill weigh hay for Mr. Coursen, taped shoes &c, dull & raw wind

—Sun 30th At home the bugle horn Naught[1] stayed here last night, quite high, tolerable pleasant

—Quite rainy, I made ax handles & made rake handles &c.

—2d I split wood again, pleasant

—3d Squally & high N.W. wind B. Dyer came over to hew some timber for me but too windy, I finished splitting wood, cold & freezeing before night

—4th A snow storm this morning, very sudden change, & snowd a part of the fore noon made an axeltree some sunshine in afternoon.

—5th I weighed hay for I. Coursen & one ton for Amos Davis, rather cool, I assisted our folks in soap making &c. went to school meeting

—Sun. 6th I went to meeting serm by Mr Hussey his second sabbath on a new engagement, muddy & bad traveling

—7 I went down to S. Nichols & got coal for E. Colby, very raw & chilly S.W. wind going down & some soft snow comeing home, very muddy, I got cob meal[2] ground at Factory

—8th Rain storm to day, made cart tongue & set & whet NJs saws

---

1 Was Naught a person who played the bugle? More likely TJ was being humorous. This is Naught's only appearance in the journal

2 "Cob meal" consists of ground corn cobs. Interestingly one of the examples of usage quoted by the OED is the following "1882 *Maine Board Agric. Rep.* XXVI. 255 Cob meal or middlings might be substituted for clear corn meal". Given cattle's ability to digest cellulose, it is nutritious fodder.

Webster April Wednesday 9th 1845

Quite a snow last night & clear this morning with very high N.W. wind, cold & the snow flies merrily a little while in the morning, I made N. Jordan a crooked yoke & steamed[1] & spread a cart tongue

—10 I put cart tongue & axeltree together put on wheels, body & Some fine snow in fore noon, more pleasant in afternoon

—11th I hauld up some wood prepared for schoolhouse, some hemlock buts[2] to the door, chopd & split them & split oven wood in fore noon & got iron work at E. Colbys in afternoon, very cold at night

—12th Froze very hard last night, I went down to the mill early & got my logs down to the slip[3], and put dogs[4] &c in an axeltree for our new wheels, put them together, body on &c & partly made a stone drag[5]

—Sun 13th The sun rose clear, soon clouds up & began to snow about noon & comes down nicely, Ann & Elizabeth is up to Clough school—house to meeting, I must needs go after them. April has been very rough so far with chilly damp S.W. wind with snow or rain, & high North West wind about all the time, not a calm, warm, pleasant sunshining day yet, direct reverse of last year. Cutters store burnt on the night of 9th

---

1 TJ often used boiling or steaming to to shape wood, as here, and in making bows for oxen yokes.

2 "buts" seem to have been synonymous with the large end of anything—trees, corn, bean stalks, etc..

3 While "slip" usually refers to an inclined ramp leading to water, TJ was probably referring to a ramp where logs were held prior to sawing.

4 "dogs" refer to device used for gripping something; here probably for attaching the axle to the cart.

5 A "stone drag" was a horse- or ox-drawn flat-bottomed skidding device, also known as a "stone sled." Often used in New England's to haul stones out of rocky fields to be used for "stone fences" (*i.e.*, stone walls), or other purposes.

Webster April Monday 14th 1845

—I finished stone drag in forenoon & made a yoke in afternoon, yesterdays snow all gone

—15th I went down to the mill, came home& hew'd out sills for a hay rack[1] in fore noon & haul'd boards joists &c. from the mill in afternoon, muddy & hard wheeling

—16th I hauld stuff from mill again & had a serious affair with our steers, desperate temper & almost ungovernable[2]

—17th Anual fast[3] I yoked our steers again & put a ring in the near ones nose. & after some resistance he yielded, & managed the cart very well, the principal trouble yesterday. I sawd some slats for fence in afternoon

—18th I helped J. Bryent repair tub wheel to grist[4]mill, dull raw unpleasant weather, B. Dyer got hurt some

—19th B. Dyer helpd me hew some timber after the morning some little snow then

—Sun 20th snowd all day, dissolved as soon as down J. Davis John Woodbury gave us a call

—21st & 22d in fore noon we hewd timber and finished, afternoon I hauld Mr. Moulton half cord wood hauld boards from the mill quite warm & pleasant

—23d I went to Topsham, very pleasant & drying, traveling rather rough

---

1 "Hay rack" may refer either to an open rack that holds hay for horses or cattle, or a wagon with a large open rack for transporting hay. TJ was probably referring to the former here.

2 Oxen are worked in pairs. The "near" or "nigh" ox, in this case a steer, is the animal on the left, the one on the right is the "off" ox. The driver always works from the left, hence the terminology. Training oxen requires time and patience.

3 "In some New England States…the day appointed every spring by the governor for fasting." OED

4 A tub wheel is a form of water-wheel. "Grist" refers to corn that is to be, or has just been ground.

Webster April Thursday 24th 1845

—I went to Factory Ville & got some boards of Peter Charles, some rain in fore noon, warm & pleasant in afternoon, I stuck up boards went to mill &c.

—25th I hauld away house banking[1] & hauld stones out of the field & left them back of the wood house

—26th I split up some ovenwood I went to Four Corners & got some work done at Colbys & split some stone out of the ledge east of the house

——Sun 27th Dull at home

—28th I piled up oven wood & hauld the stone mentioned above to the wood house & dug up corn buts on a piece[2] in the N.W. corner of the field, I went up to Josep[h] Chadbourns & over to Charles Hinkleys land to look at stone for underpinning,[3]

—29th I was at work on a cart body for E. Jordan 2d some rain in fore noon & pleasant in afternoon

—30th I harrowd corn ground in fore noon by pasture wall & got off corn buts[4] I harrowd for wheat in afternoon

—May first. I and Jesse Davis having had a summons yesterday went up to Rushwith Fickits in a case or trial on a petition for an increase of damages in consequence of the location of a County road from [continued on next page]

---

1 "banking"refers to earth used to pile around the foundation of a house in the winter as a form of insultation.

2 TJ uses the term "piece" many times in his journal. At the time "piece" meant (among other things) a "plot of land" with the connotation of it being in some way bounded. OED

3 "underpinning": material used to support a building; *i.e*, a foundation.

4 The dried stalk and root remaining after the corn was harvested.

Lewiston to the Potter road so called, The Jury did not arrive in season to proceed to business on account of some misunderstanding of the place of meeting Willson the County Attorney attached blame to the high Sheriff & Saml. Moody, Esq.[1]

—2d We attended in afternoon at Mr. Fickets but the Jury had not arrived from the eastern end of the road——we had quite a squall about noon; the house & barn of Peter Freeman in Greene was burnt on evening of 30th ult

—3d We attended a[t] Fickets again & found the Jury & whole posse on the ground & proceeded to view S. Dyers land at the road on his land, went over the same & repaired to Fickets for a hearing, when a smoke was discovered in a southerly direction from sd [said] Fickets, soon after news came that the buildings of D.L. Weymouth were on fire whereupon we left without much ceremony for the place & on arriving we found it but too true, for barn where the fire was first discovered the house cornbarn woodhouse & all was burned to the ground, together with one horse two calves one swine farming utensils &c considerable furniture saved

---

1 TJ usually refers to lawyers as esquires (or Esq.)

Webster May 1845

Nothing taken from the cellar & a great loss in the house—J. Davis had a very providential in the wind changing from N. or N W. to west soon after the fire was discovered—not known how the fire originated—Capt. & I returned to Feckts.

—Sun. 4th At meeting at fourcorners
—5th I harrowd for wheat in fore noon in NW corner of the fiel[d] Afternoon S. Coursen[1] helped me finish plowing a piece of green sward[2] in eastern field & harrowd on the same the remainder of afternoon

—7th I sowd two bushels wheat & harrowd it in, I was calld away in afternoon to stop fire on west side of mountain set by Wm Coursen, Amazing dry & every day windy

—8th I met Jacob Herrick & Peter Charles on the premises of Auletus Philips & David B. Frost on a warrant from Court to set off & assign to D. Frost one half of sd premises in quantity & quality spent the day in viewing the premises & appearing before Justice Moody to take an oath of division, some snow this morning & very cold all day[3]

---

1 The Coursens were neighbors whose sons—usually Samuel—frequently helped TJ, presumably as hired farm hands.

2 "sward" refers to grassy ground

3 TJ was frequently called to survey land and act as a referee when property needed to be divided.

Webster May 9th 1845

Met at David B. Frosts again, proceeded to survey sd farm & chain[1] out the same did not get through very cold & windy

—10th Met again & completed the division, set off & assigned David B. Frost the eastern side of sd. Farm excepting fifteen or twenty acres in N.W. corner of sd farm; very cold raw wind

—Sun 11th very pleasant & quite warm

—12th S. Coursen helpd me haul out manure, very fine

—13th E. Jordan 2d helpd me haul manure & plow for corn, still pleasant

—14th I sow'd some peas & oats & barley, Mary Ann went to Brunswick, fine

—15th I harrowd broke up land for corn in fore noon & went over to J.B. Jordans in afternoon on a committee with P.M. Garcelon of the part of the town & John Williams on the part of Oran Gillpatrick to settle certain claims the the sd Gillpatrick pretend to hold against the town in consequence of the small pox in 1841 Committee decided that sd Gillpatrick should have twelve [dollars] allowed on his bill of sixty nine[2] some little sprink[l]e of rain in morning & quite a rain in afternoon with some thunder wind N.E.

— 16th E. Jordan helpd me plow, cold & windy

---

1 The length of a surveying chain was standardized in 1624 as 66 feet. A parcel ten chains in length by one chain wide equals one acre

2 We may assume that Gillpatrick provided some service during a smallpox epidemic in 1841. Possibly he vaccinated the town's inhabitants. Edward Jenner (1749-1823) had published *An Inquiry into the Causes and Effects of the Variolae Vaccinae, a Disease Known by the Name of Cow Pox* in 1798. Benjamin Waterhouse (1754-1846) introduced vaccination into the United States the following year. Its value was recognized immediately—Thomas Jefferson even sent cowpox matter west with the Lewis and Clark expedition in 1803 for vaccinating Indians (unfortunately the vaccine was inactive). That an epidemic occurred four decades later in rural Maine shows that it still was not in general use.

Webster May Saturday 17th 1845

I cross harrowed sward land old ground for corn & finshd a cart body for E. Jordan 2d some rain afternoon & a great rain at night

—Sun. 18th Very rainy in fore noon the ground well soaked by this time, having been ucommon dry since the spring opened. Mr. & Mrs. Hinkley up here since the 13th

—19th I got flat stone on Wm Jordans hill & hauld them home

—2oth Wm & sam Coursen helpd me put out manure for corn

—21st I covered corn all day

—22d & 23d Ivory Coursen helpd me plant corn & finshd

—24th I hauld one thousand brick from J. Durgins

—Sun. 25th We were up to Mr. Dyers

—25, 27 , 28, 29 & 30th planting potatoes principally.

31st I put out manure for beans & prepared ground & sowd carrots

—Sun June 1st. At meeting four Corners

—2d I harrowd ground & finished planting potatoes

 —3 & 4 I & Henry Jordan split stone over on Charles Hinkly land, very warm indeed

—5th 6th & 7th at work on Highway, had a shower of hailstones on 5th.

Aaron Davis house burnt on 6th high westerly wind

Sun 8 up to B Dyers & A. Davis, some rain in morning but pleasant in afternoon

Webster June 9th 1845

Reuben Dyer began work with me for half a month, we washed sheep in the morning & planted beans in the field & garden & mangelwortsel &c in garden

—10th We started early & hauld one load of stone from C. Hs [Charles Hinkley] very warm & dry—we cleared out woodhouse hog pen &c. in order to move wood house & put up a portch[1] between house & woodhouse. I got another load of stone in afternoon

—12th Reuben & I went over after another load of stone with four wheels & Mr Robinsons oxen, quite early & another in afternoon. James Farrow shearing our sheep today, a little rain this morning, clearing woodhouse &c..

—12th We cleared out & hauld manure from hog pen into cow yard, hauld away stone hauld up timber ground axes &c.

—13th B. Dyer Reuben & I began to frame the portch, very warm & growing indeed having had a very fine & seasonable rain indeed last night

—14th A smart rain in fore noon, did not work at framing , cleard off in afternoon, we began to dig out for a cistern

—Sun 15th Very fine & pleasant, did not go to meeting, sleeping & tired Vegetation comes forward rapidly

---

1 "portch" at that time implied a utility room on the rear of a house. TJ's spelling was correct as "portch" is the spelling used at the time. New England farmhouses tended to get strung out as structures were added.

Webster Monday June 16th 1845

More rain last night, Moved woodhouse to day, finished framing & raised the new portch, fine day

———17th More rain again went down to see H. Jordan about underpining portch & Mr. Atwood about building cistern &c. hauld sand clay &c.

—18th H. Jordan underpined portch

—19th I & B Dyer boarded roof put on lead[1] & shingled house side

—20th Mr. Atwood & son began to build cistern

—21st finished cistern & boiler chimney[2]

—22d fine day at home, I heard yesterday that Aaron Crowley had asconded with the wife of one Chenery of Falmouth.

—23rd Hoed corn, Ivory Coursen, Sam & James helping R. Dyers half month out to day

—24th B. Dyer came and began to shingle portch

—25th Shingling

—26th finishd & boarded portch, very high drying wind—I got out stuff for windows frames in fore noon & helpd D L Weymouth raise a barn frame in afternoon

—27th boarded portch, put on face boards &c.

—28th Pried up woodhouse, set stone under posts & sills put sleepers[3] in portch got out door stuff &c.

---

1 Lead flashing was used below the bottom course of shingles for water run-off and along the peak where top courses of shingles meet.

2 TJ's cistern would have been a well-like water reservoir probably located above the house to provide running water. Mr. Atwood presumably was a stone mason

3 "sleepers" are horizontal weight-bearing beams to which floor boards are nailed.

Webster Sunday June 29th 1845

At home all day A. Davis & wife here last night & to day, rather cool nights

—30th At work for B. Dyer splitting stone, cold & raw N E. wind

—July 1st R. Dyer helpd me hoe potatoes, I mended rakes for B. Carvill, cold & cloudy

—2d We hoed potatoes again in forenoon, dull & began to rain about noon, quite rain[y] in P.M. I plained clapboards

— 3rd Very rainy I plained clapboards again the ground is well soaked

—4th Fine & pleasant. I hauled flat stone from Mr. Robinsons hill & went down to S McGray's to see D. McFarland engaged him to work on portch & engaged Henry Jordan to underpin wood house to morrow

—5th H. Jordan help'd underpin woodhouse very fine weather

—Sun 6th We went to funeral of Aaron Clark who died on 4th very large meeting, quite warm.

—7th I went down after Mr McFarland early, he cased doors & I hauld dirt to fill round underpining & cistern

—8th I hauld some dirt, hauld some boards & layed portch floor &c

—9th I hoed garden, finishd hoeing potatoes by Factory road & hoed some beans

Webster Thursday July 10th 1845

I finised hoeing beans & at work round the portch pointing[1] underpining &c

—11th I hauled manure & muck into yard & finishd hoeing potatoes & corn the second time by the help of S. Coursen E. Jordan R Dyer & Silas Jordan, appearance of rain in fore noon but fine & warm in afternoon

—12th We layed portch floor or a part of it in fore noon Mr McFarland went home at noon & I finishd laying the floor painted doors &c in afternoon

—13th Dull & some little rain in the morning not at meeting rather stupid[2]

—14th & 15th Dull at work with Mr. McFarland on the portch

—16th I mowed some very warm

—17th Dull at work in garden all day

—18th Mowed some more, very fine hay day

b—19th Mowed some by Factory road

—Sun 20th Dull at home

—21st Reuben Dyer & Wm. Coursen helpd me

—23 Dull had showers in afternoon General Blossoms buildings burnt by lightning[3]

—24 R. Dyer & I put up hog pen at end of wood house

—25th & 26th Mr Coursen helpd us

— 27th At funeral of Dea[con] David Pettingills wife some rain

---

1 "pointing" means to fill in joint or cracks in masonry with mortar or cement.

2 The term "stupid" did not have the meaning of mental deficiency that it does today; TJ probably meant "apathetic" or "indifferent," or just plain tired out.

3. General Blossom not identified.

Webster Monday July 28th 1845

Mowed the round knowl & swamp by the little bridge

—29th C. Jordan 2d helpd us fair hay day & fair prospect, left hay in winrow[1]

—30th I got up early & great prospect of rain, rolled up some hay & began to rain early , quite rainy all day. & had a very heavy shower in evening & morning of 31st but clears off in forenoon & warm too I carried Mr. McFarland home at noon, he having workd three days this week, ten & half days in all

—Aug 1st & 2d Mr Coursen helpd us & we mowed the new grass below sweet apple trees & easterly got in new grass
2d in fine order

—Sun 3d Dull again we unloaded two carts & got in one load of hay in fore noon, quite fair in afternoon, Niah H. & wife up here, fair prospect of fair weather in evening, poor & uneven hay weather so far, but here I must say that the late rain is glorious for fall feed & vegetation in general & more we are all blessed with tolerable health & enough to eat & drink & employment enough for our hands
4th Quite fair hay day except a wind squall & shower just before night
Wm & James Coursen helping

---

1 After it is cut, hay is raked into rows to dry.

Webster Thursday August 5th 1845

Very fine hay day[1] got in six load

—Fine again got in three load

—rather poor hay day but very warm in fore noon & Jordan 2d helpd & nearly finished mowing in fore noon & very fine finished mowing & got all in

—9th Excessive hot I went to Brunswick after cement did not obtain it—sick of relax[2]

—Sun 10th went to meeting at four corners serm[on] by Mr. Hussey, warm but more air to day

—11, 12, 13th Making preparations to plaster portch, lathing slacking lime &c[3] I sent to Portland by W. Jordan & got a barrrel of cement on 12th

—15 & 16th John Atwood plastered portch, cistern, topd out chimnney & layed hearth &c Sally was taken quite ill on 15th cancer broke out[4]

—Sun 17th Much company Lucy Farrow & others

—18th & 19 Daniel Ames cradled our wheat we got it all shockd[5]

—20, 21, 22 & 23d I painted portch raked wheat stubble & at work around portch &c some rain

—Sun 24th I went to meeting in afternoon & down on the ridge to get a girl to help us

—25 I reap a little wheat & mowed barley & peas & oats, got in grass seed &c

—26 Got in barley & peas & oats

—27th & 28th Meeting of the Kennebec Association of Universalist at four corners[6]

---

1 A "fine hay day" would be sunny and dry, a day on which the mowed grass would dry into hay quickly.

2 It is unclear what TJ meant by this; "relax" was a noun as well as a verb; it meant "relaxation."

3 Plastering involved nailing horizontal lathes to the studding, then applying plaster. The latter consisted of slaked lime and sand. Usually horse-hair was added to hold the plaster together.

4 Sally was TJ's older sister, his parent's second child. I do not have her birthdate but would assume that she was about 50. Almost certainly the condition was cancer of the breast.

5 TJ was mowing by hand using a scythe with a rake-like device or "cradle" that caught the grain and laid it neatly in the mower's swath so it could be gathered into bundles

Webster Tuesday August 29th 1845

I went up to Lewiston to get Mary Carvill but did not get her, she being at work in Danvill, went down to S. McGray's & engaged Betsy Ford, I threshed grass seed[1] in afternoon

—30th S. Coursen helpd me thresh peas & oats, dull, southerly wind

—Sun. 31st Very fine day I carried R. Dyer home or up to J. Lowels & went over to Auburn to meeting in afternoon

—Sept. 1st At work on the road, fine day

—2d At work on road in fore noon, some rain & quite rainy in afternoon

—3d I went to mill B's water too low to get ground then went Factory clears off in afternoon I pulld peas &c

—4th I cut & hauld sleepers for hog pen in the morning, opend wheat[2] & got it into the barn in afternoon

—5th I went up after B. Dyer early, we hewd sleepers for hog pen layed floor & boarded outer pen &c

—6th finshd floor shingled roof put up hogs &c &c I carried B. Dyer home in evening

—Sun 7th Quite rainy

—8th I cut & hauld out gutter poles[3] & fitted pigs trough, & put up pigs &c in fore noon & went to election of state officers in afternoon, Jacob Hill chosen representative, I pulled some beans in the garden

---

1 Threshing implies separating seed from its seed cover and stalk. Although TJ later uses a threshing machine for his wheat he probably used a flail to separate the grass seed from the dried hay so that he could collect it and use for sowing at a later time.

2 Probably when TJ "opend wheat" he removed it from the shocks

3. Long straight poles that could be partly hollowed out to use for gutters.

("shocks") to ripen further and dry. Horse drawn mowing machines soon became available

6 The Universalist Society was founded in the United States by clergyman John Murray (1741-1814). "Universalism" was a liberal religious creed based on Christian principles (the name came from the belief that God was one and not a trinity). Although universalism originated in England, the Society was American, and was well represented in New England, where Murray had lived and preached. The Universalist Society was closely related to the Unitarian church and the two entities merged in 1961 to become the Unitarian Universalist Association.

Webster Tuesday Sept. 9th 1845

I cut stalk in fore noon, Saml Coursen helping commenced work by the month, dug some potatoes, pulld beans & tied up stalks in afternoon, potatoes rotting in the hill is general complaint

—10th We hauld dirt to fill up wood house in forenoon & cut stalks in afternoon—Sally is so smart[1] as to be down stairs & out door

—11th I cut & tied up stalk in fore noon & hauld in beans in afternoon, very fine

—12th I shookd[2] stalks & cut up corn in fore noon & dug potatoes in afternoon

—13th I cut corn in fore noon & shooked in afternoon & set brush on fire in evening, very pleasant indeed until just before night, then clouds up

—Sun. 14th Moderate rain the most of the day

—15th to 20th I made spouts to conduct water into the cistern—set the pump, lead &c dug potatoes, hauld dirt into the woodhouse[3] cleared staging of portch &c. &c

—21st I went up to Amos Davis & brought home Elizabeth[4]

—22d dug potatoes in fore noon & afternoon I killd lambs[5]

—23rd I went to Topsham to market, & got threshing machine[6] at Josep[h] Blethens at night

—24th Began to thresh our wheat

—25th finishd

---

1 In this context "smart" means "to have strength."

2 "shookd": TJ means "bundled" or "shocked.

3 Probably for the floor.

4 Elizabeth was TJ's and Mary Ann's second oldest child (30 August 1832 -11 April 1861); she would have been 13 at this time.

5 TJ will slaughter livestock all through the fall. There usually was not enough food to carry animals through the long Maine winter, so farmers kept only as many as they needed for breeding.

6 Hiram and John Pitts of Winthrop, Maine, patented a threshing machine in 1837, operated by horsepower. Probably this was the threshing machine that TJ used. Prior to this wheat was separated from its straw and husks by beating with flails and collecting the grain.

Webster Friday Sept 26th 1845

I winnowed wheat[1] 36 bushels S. Coursen helping N Jordan

—27th I hauld pumkins & three load corn, E Colby jun came here with a man professing to have the art of cureing cancers, Sally engaged him to cure hers, to come again on 29th inst.[2]

—Sun 28th Tolerable pleasant

—29th I dug potatoes & finishd pink eyes[3] by the road

—30th We dug red potatoes up by the side of the corn

—October first Quite rainy, We husked out the corn we had in sorted & put in the crib & cleared the old corn out of the other crib &c.

—2d Got in stalks &cc

—3d Got in topd corn & some of shook

—4th Got in the last of the shookd in fore noon & had a number of the neighbors to help us husk in the evening

—Sun 5 dull

—6th Rainy husked & sorted corn

—7th I helped N. Jordan split stone

—8 do. Very pleasant days

—9th Rainy finished sorting corn

—11th I mended my boots &c

—13th I went over & helpd N Jordan put irons on stump machine in fore noon—& dug some potatoes in afternoon

—14th dug potatoes

—15 very cold hauld dung

—16 Hauld some dung & dug potatoes

—17 & 18 Dug potatoes

—19 went to meeting

---

1 To winnow is to separate the chaff and other small particulate matter from the wheat kernels. It was usually carried out by tossing the wheat while a wind was blowing allowing the light chaff to be carried off; the word "winnow" is derived from "wind."

2 In a day when medical practice was unregulated, "cancer doctors" and other quacks often preyed on the sick and desperate. Sally's doctor, J.S. Mudget prescribed for her, apparently, on this visit.

3 "pink-eye": A variety of potato having pink eyes or buds. OED.

Webster Oct Monday 20th 1845

Helped D.L. Weymouth raise a part of his house in fore noon &
finishd diging potatoes same day unwell & lame hand

—21 & 22d I made an axel tree to Wentworth Jordan's waggon

—23 & 24th I got garden sauce[1] & hauld dung

—25th I went to Factory to mill & spread dung on grass below hard
sweet appletrees to plow in

— Sun pleasant

—27 & 28 E. Jordan 2d helpd me plow

—29 30 & 31 Silas & Reuben Dyer helpd me plow in the old pasture
from the field to old house [so] calld afternoon of 31, got wood in
wood house &[c]

—November 1 hauld out the last of yard manure, very unusually warm
the past week

—Sun 2d Dull but moderate, some rain in afternoon,

—3d very rainy all day & night

—4 Powerful rain in fore noon I went to Factoryvill in afternoon to
mill, but water too high to get [the wheat] ground a great freshet &
went up to Lombards mill, got home in evening soon after had a very
heavy shower with thunder & lightning

—5 Still thick & wind out this morning I made some stye bows[2] &
fixed roof of wood house to prevent a leak at end of portch

---

1 "garden sauce" refers to garden vegetables and various greens.

2 I am uncertain as to the meaning of "stye bows." "Sty" is an archaic word for "ladder,"
and, given that TJ was roofing, it might have meant ladder rungs. It may also, of course,
simply referred to a pig pen.

Webster Thursday Nov. 6th 1845

I threshed beans, quite pleasant & mild went up to Clough's school house to a temperance meeting in evening

—7th Winnowed beans peas &c

—8th I went to Factoryville & got a load of tan[1] to put over the cistern & got some board came on to rain soon afternoon—quite rainy all the afternoon & evening

—Sun. 9th Rainy again all day, very moderate for the season and very wet

—10th Rainy tapd Anns shoes & cut & closed Elizabeth a pr

—11th I made Elizabeth's shoes, clear & pleasant, I killd two sheep to carry to Bath tomorrow

—12th I started for Bath in fore noon, dull & thick, clears off pleasant in afternoon

—13th Sold butter, apples, beans & mutton &c and got home

—14th I finishd the end of portch & partly made a door to shut out side of back door, Mr Robinson & wife here in evening

—15th I hung sd door, made & put up a gutter to back side of portch &c &c, and went to mill in evening at Lombards. Capt. Jesse Davis & wife made us a visit in evening

—Sun 16th At meeting sermon by Mr. French, very moderate weather yet

---

1 "tan" or "tan-bark" was ground bark used to tan leather. The spent bark was used much like peat moss in gardening, on horse trails, and traditionally under circus tents.

Webster Monday Nov. 17th 1845

I went to Topsham & carried Mrs. Perkins a firkin[1] of butter for which I got one shilling[2] per lb. Major P. sick with small pox. Three young men belonging to Topsham rode off of a bridge or the abutment of a brid[g]e last night & got injured very much very warm & pleasant

—18th Rainy all day I got an hogshead of [?] P.M. Garcelon & got some sand & pumped water out of cistern in order to find & stop the leak, sodered lead pipe &c.

—19th I hauld home threshing machine from N. J.s & hauld some dirt in forenoon, & cleaning out cistern &c in afternoon & went down to Niah Hs. in evening to get him to butcher our hogs tomorrow

—20th We started early & got underway & killd one hog & a pig in fore noon the pig having had both thighs broke last evening. The cause not known & a hog & a pig in afternoon, the hogs weighing 546 —525 lb & pigs 170 lb each[3]

—21st some little rain in morning, but clear & moderate the remainder of the day, I cut up & salted pork

—22d I made fence & bridge for pigs to get to sty, & hauld some stone away & banked house &c, &c

---

1 A small barrel-like container, about a quarter of a barrel in size.

2 One of the OED's citations from 1891 notes that "reckoning by the shilling is still not uncommon in some parts of the United States, especially in rural New England." The shilling had different value in various countries; *e.g.*, in England, 1 shilling = 12 pence. On the basis of TJ's subsequent sale of farm goods, I would guess that a shilling would be worth about 10 cents.

3 One would think that "pigs is pigs", but "hog," as TJ used the term, meant a castrated male pig raised for slaughter, and a pig was "the young of swine, male or female." OED.

Webster Sunday Nov. 23d 1845

Strong southerly wind this morning & thick not withstanding it being so pleasant last evening & wind northerly, quite rainy in afternoon & evening quite a remarkable fall, so wet & warm J.S Mudget here again on 21st left more gum and gave directions for curing Sally's cancer[1]

—24th Hauld dirt to bank house & the front of new portch in fore noon & went up to Greene in afternoon after a buck, very cold & freezeing

—25th Got wood in wood house pried up stone, set stone under shed post & sawed bunks[2] &c &c

—26th chop'd wood in woods, thick[3] at night

—27th Quite rainy all day & tremenduous wind in afternoon. Blew away many buildings, I made Holman a pair shoes & the first [?]

—28th Making a pair shoes for S. Coursen in fore noon & helpd E Jordan 2d on a barn door in afternoon, rather cool

—29th I finishd S. Coursen's shoes & helpd E. Jordan 2d again in afternoon

—30th Great appearance of snow in morning but holds off till night & then fell 4 or 5 in.

—Dec 1st Snowed a little in morning and then turns to rain & rains smartly in afternoon, I was at work on a pr of boots for myself

—2d I finishd boots clear & cold

---

1 TJ mentioned on September 27th that a man was coming to see Sally. In the front of his diary on an unlined fly leaf he had also written "John S. Mudget, Lebanon Maine Cancer Doctor Sept.29th 1845." From this distance it is hard to guess which of several plant gums (probably plant sap or extract) with known antineoplastic activity Mudget might have prescribed. An intriguing possibility would be resin obtained from the root of the may-apple *Podophylum peltatum*, a plant found throughout the Northeast. The active ingredient, podophyllin, is still used medicinally—and effectively—in the treatment of venereal warts, a virus-induced neoplasm. The Penobscot Indians of Maine are known to have used the root of the may-apple to treat cancer (Lewis, W.F. and M.P.F. Lewis, *Medical Botany*, NY, John Wiley & Sons, 1977). More recently, systemically administered podophyllin has been shown to have anti-neoplastic activity, although its toxicity prohibits general use. TJ does not mention whether Sally used Dr. Mudget's gum internally or topically. I suspect the latter in view of his note that "Sally was taken quite ill on 15th [August, 1845] cancer broke out." There is also a suggestion that she might have used it internally—see note below for Dec. 19, 1845.

2 A bunk was a "piece of wood placed on a lumberman's sled to enable it to sustain the end of heavy pieces of timber." *Maine U.S.* Bartlett." OED These were probably side stakes, as TJ also uses the word "bunk" for fence posts.

3 "thick," means mist, haze, or fog—most likely the last.

Webster Wednesday Dec 3 1845

—S. Coursen helpd me chop in the woods, very cold

—4th Thanksgiving[1] —we killd a beef cow in fore noon & chop in woods in afternoon, quite a snow storm all day, but some rain at night

—I went down to Factoryville. & carried down one hind quarter of beef weighing 116 lb & sold it to Weinal & Lebbe for 3[?] cents per lb & left it for John Atwood Jun. Afternoon killd three sheep

—6th I went to Topsham sold mutton for 2 1/2 cents & roasting pieces for 6 cts per lb quite cool got oxen shod[2]

—8th I sold J. Wagg three bushel beans for $1.50 per bushel,

—9th Some rain

—10th I went over to four corners & up to B. Dyer's, cut up & salted beef &c

11th & 12th chopd wood again, very cold

13th Very pleasant indeed I got nails drawd from ox hoof & hauld flat stone to make fence by Factory road

—Sun 14 some snow

—15th rain & damp snow

—16th I went into the woods with team, the swamp much overflowed & high wind Amos Davis & wife here

—17th I went over to the town farm[3] in Lewiston to get Abigail Merrill to come & work with us, found her at home & came home with me to take care of Sally who is very sick

7th We went to B. Hams funeral, cold

---

1 Thanksgiving Day had been celebrated in December until President Franklin Roosevelt changed the date to the 4th Thursday in November, in 1941.

2 Unlike U-shaped shaped horseshoes, oxen shoes were shaped like a pair of parentheses to fit the cleft hooves.

3 A farm maintained by the community for orphans and the indigent; *i.e.*, a poor-farm.

Webster Thursday Dec. 18th 1845

I chopd wood in woods, very moderate

—19th I went over to four Corners to get some rum for Sally[1] & bought an ax & put an handle in the same in for noon & at work in woods in afternoon, moderate & snow soft —20th I put bobsled[2] together &c in fore noon & E Jordan 2d help'd me [haul?] some pine logs &c in afternoon, cooler

—Sun 21st. Some spits of snow I went up to B Dyer in afternoon, Mrs Dyer is much better than shw was one year since—brought Reuben home to help me load wood

—22d & 23d & 24th Hauled wood, fine weather & good sledding hauld fifteen load

—25th & 26th Thick weather some little snow, hauld wood again[3]

—27th Fine again, hauld wood in fore noon, I hauld wood for Wm Wentworth in afternoon

—28th did not go to meeting, Ann, Elizabeth, & Mary Dyer went in fore noon

—29 & 30th We hauld wood & finish all that we had chop'd

—31st We hauld fencing to fence the piece plowed in the pasture in fore noon & broke two axes & ground them in afternoon, cold & windy

January 1st 1846 Hauld fencing again more moderate, clouds up for a storm

---

1 Sally was clearly very ill from her cancer, from the "gum" given her by Dr. Mudget, or both, and obviously in pain. Mudget might better have given her opium, for which rum is a poor substitute. (Reflect a bit and imagine the implications of cancer and other serious illness in those times.)

2 A bobsled consisted of two short sleds joined together to make it more maneuverable than a longer one would be; used for hauling timber and carrying other heavy loads.

3 TJ does not mention Christmas, although later in the journal he does note a Christmas celebration (see entry for Sunday, January 8, 1849). English puritans banned Christmas in 1644 and their influence extended to the Ameican colonies. It did not become an important holiday, especially in the northern United States, until German immigrants and others made it so in the 19th Century. (*Encyclopaedia Brittanica*, 11th Ed., NY 1910.)

Webster Friday January 2nd 1846

Quite stormy in fore noon light snow & rain in afternoon. I've repaired bobsled, whet fine saw for B. Dyer & whetted my own, & repaired wash tub &c.

—3d Some rain early this morning but none after, we chopd poles for fencing by the brook, snow quite soft, grows cooler at night

—Sun. 4th Cool & pleasant. Mary Ann & Holmon went up to B. Dyers with Reuben

—5th Went into the woods to haul fencing, early, I let William Jordan have our horse to go to Portland

—6th Hauld fencing again

—7th Snow storm all day, John Jordan from Cape Elizabeth came here

—8th Some snow in fore noon & broke road into he woods in afternoon snow quite deep

— 9th I carried children to school on ox sled & went to mill & Wentworth & wife here in fore noon did not go into the woods in afternoon

—10th Hauld fencing in fore noon & carried pig over to Aaron Goodwins In afternoon

—11th Dull Reuben Dyer went home & carred Rebecca home—12th hauld fencing, N. Js young folks here in evening

—13th I went up to Joseph Blethens in Company Wm Garcelon & John Carvill & commenced upon the task of making a division of the Jone's farm between Joseph Blethen & Rufus Sibley surveyed said farm & found it to contain very near 175 acres

14th & 15th engaged in that bisiness & completed the division to the acceptance of parties

—16th We went to the S. W. Bend shopping

—17th Some stormy

—Sun 18 Clear & cold

—19th Very cold Nathan Jordan from Newportland & Sully Jordan from Cape Elizabeth came here at evening

—20th More pleasant I picked over some potatoes took care of cattle &c.

—21st I hauld some fencing

— 22d Very cold and windy went up to Lombards mill

—23d I chored round the house

—24th I hauld stuff for pole fence quite moderate

—Sun. 25th Clear & wind north & west & very smart breeze & still thaws considerable, Mary Ann went down to see Mrs Davis who is quite low & declines daily & over to N. Jordans who had a young daughter last night

—26th I Hauld fencing thick & some snow in afternoon & evening— S. Storer from Harpswell up at night

—27th Very fine & pleasant, finisheed hauling fencing & hauld some large hemlock logs. Mudget calld today. Sally is quite feeble

Webster Wednesday Jan. 28th 1846

I cut a stick[1] for sled runners but proved hollow in fore noon & cut an old dead hemlock in afternoon

—29th I chopd wood at the door, Ann, Sally Jordan & Drusilla Dyer went up to John Pettingills

—30th I sorted taters dull.

—31st I carried Drusilla D. home in fore noon & picked over potatoes in afternoon

—Sun. Feb 1st Clear & pleasant fine weather, I was into Mr. Marrs in afternoon

—2d I chored around house in for noon & hauld logs to the mill in afternoon, very fine

—3d I hauld one load of logs to the mill & did nothing more Rufus Libby & wife here—I shelld some corn in evening.

—4th I carried our wood down to Mr Corbet for which he payed me 30 cts per bl. I paid J. Durgin two dollars, all that I owed him—paid J. Atwood Jun. fifty cents, all that was due him, I then went over to Stephen Goulds & then up to Dr. Garcelon & paid him five dollars & three cents——$3.69 that I owed him & $1.34 that Sally owed him, then got my papers[?] & came home, Rebecca & Eunice Gould up here, very pleasant some thawy

—5th I cut & hauld a pair of sled runners or stick to make them

---

1 The word "stick" was in common use at the time, referring to the trunk of a tree.

Webster Friday Feb 6th 1846

I went to Topsham, & got two casks lime & 112 lbs iron [for sled runners] fine day

—7th I went into the woods & got an elm for sled bars & bored sled runners apart.[1] dull all day

—Sun 8th Cold & snow drifting considerable

—9th I hauld out sled bars

—10th I went up to Wm Maxwells with team & hauld down a load of timber for E. Jordan 2d, cold grey day & some snow

—11th & 12th At work on the sled as above

—12 at evening we went up to Mr Robinsons on a visit, quite cold

—13th Very blustering snow drifts merrily—I went after the children at school & carried Mr Wentworths children & Joshua Jordans home Almond Wilkins of Green got blockaded & stopd with us at night.

—14th I shoveled out the road some & carried the children to school, had trouble with our cistern pump, having not wholly run down and froze in the lead[2], at work on the sled &c

—Sun 15th Very cold gray day I went over to Dr Garcelons to get some medicine for Sally & P.M. G[arcelon]s & got spirit, biscuit &c.

—16th I hewd out sled tongue, and went down to Niah Hinkleys in evening—J.L. Davis wife is very sick not expected to live but a very short time.

---

1 separately .

2 Lead pipe. The Jordan's plumbing apparently consisted of diverting water into the cistern that TJ had constructed the previous summer. Water was then pumped through lead pipes into the house. Lead pipes were in general use well into the first half of the 20th century when it was realized that they caused lead poisoning If the pump was not drained by elevating the pump handle after use, water remained in the pipe and froze in cold weather—a common mishap. Fortunately, malleable lead pipes seldom crack when this occurs, in the way that iron pipes do.

I put sled tongue and roller[1] together & finishd sled

—18th Chopd some wood quite pleasant. Charles Gould & wife up here

—19th Chopd & sawd wood—bought clover seed of of Garcelon of New Portland—heard that J L. Davis wife died early this morning. I went over to N.Js & got his pung[2]

—20th I went down to Bowdoinham village & got half ton plaster in the store—on my return at Carters Corner, commenced snowing & had a tough storm home & all the evening

—I broke out the road early & got the cattle out made ready & went down to J L. Davis to assist at the funeral of his wife, quite pleasant
—Sun. 22d Pleasant again

—23d I got out & put up hams chops & to smoke & sorted potatoes
—24th I got eight bushels of oats of Mr. Robinsons paid half cash and give them [?] for the other half, made division in new tyup[3] to turn cows loose to calve

—25th I carried hyde down to HI Holland to have tanned & went over to Jordans at S.W. B. [South West Bend] to make a market for bacon, had 7 1/2 cts offered could get molasses for 24 cts, quite cool, Mr Robinsons young folks here in evening—I forgot to mention that we were down to Capt Jesse Davis last evening on a visit.

---

1 The tongue was a shaft that protruded from the front of a sled, cart, or in this case a roller to which the oxen's yoke was attached. Roads were not plowed, but were rolled to give a firm surface for sleighs to glide on.

2 A pung is a light, horse drawn sleigh or sled. The word was also used for a toboggan. It was derived from the Indian term "tow-pung" from which our word "toboggan" was also derived. OED.

3 "Tie-up:" a term used in the U.S. meaning "A building or stall in which cattle are tied up for the night." OED.

Webster Feb 28th 1846

I carried bacon over to S.W.B.1 & got a barrel of molasses, poor sleighing

—Sun March 1st Very cold this morning, tending cattle cutting and sawing wood &c, &c

—6th I was making an iron ware chest.

—7th Finishd painted the same

—8th A Davis & wife here, Sally is failing gradually

—9th I cut out & closed a pair of shoes for Father

—19th Finished the above shoes John L. Jordan & Walter here & turned ox bows very pleasant

—11th I went over to S. W. B. and got oil paint &c. pleasant again

—12th I went up to Lewiston falls to get a grindstone found none very fine & snow runing merrily

—13th I was up to Joseph Blethens to help S. D. Rand rise up the old house preparatory to hauling, dull in afternoon & smart rain in the night

—14th Some rain in morning & evening, I mended shoes

—Sun 15 I carried Abigail Merrill home & got Clarrissa Mitchell at Mr. Crowleys on my return, the streams are quite high & the snow soft & slumpy[1]

——16th Reuben Dyer commenced helping chop our wood, a soft damp snow in afternoon

— 17th Dull & damp, chopd wood

---

1. South-west Bend, presumably on the Androscoggin River.

2 "slumpy": wet and boggy.

Webster March Wednesday 18th 1846

We chopd wood in fore noon & helpd S. D. Rand haul the old Jones house in afternoon, had good luck, got it on the spot without injurry

—19th Dull & some little soft snow at night, but chopd wood all day, Ann went over to Dr. G[arcelon]s & had a tooth hauld[1]

—20th very pleasant, the snow run off very much I went over to J. Thompson's in evening, poor sleighing, quite bare

—21st Quite rainy A. Davis & wife came down. Old Mr. Golder was buried yesterday & Ebenezer Dill died & is to be buried tomorrow

—Sun 22d Pleasant sun but quite windy. A. Davis & wife went home, Sally is very feeble apparantly of short stay

—23rd I went to annual town meeting Jesse Davis Saml Cushman & James Mann chosen Selectmen, Ass[e]ssors & Overseers of the poor fine day & snow runs merrily

—24th I chopd wood all day, fine again

—245h some rain I plained of cart spokes for Barramus Fish a pair of wheels

—26th B. Dyer came & we began work upon Foss wheels, rainy

—27th rainy, 28 clears up, did not finish Foss wheels

—Sun 29th Fair, great freshet[2] at this time, S.W.B. bridge went off last night

---

1 As is clear from the context, "haul"—a word used often by TJ—was synonymous with "pull."

2 While we think of a freshet as a small seasonal stream, TJ used the word to mean an overflowing river, or flood.

Webster Monday March 30th 1846

B. Dyer & I finishd Foss [?] wheels & began to make a pair for John L. Davis

—31st & April 1st 2d at work on J. D.s wheels & finished them on 3d in fore noon & I made cart axeltree for E. Jordan 2d in afternoon very fine & pleasant indeed so far this week

—4 I chopd near the last of the wood pile ~~& begun pile or tier the wood~~, very fine but southerly wind

—Sun 5th I went to meeting at four corners, serm. by Mr. West being his first serm this season & made an appointment to preach again in two weeks

—6th I weighed 1337 lb hay in fore noon for E. Jordan 2d in forenoon & then finishd chopping wood & piled up one tier, Sally is evidently failing daily.

—7th Saml. Coursen helpd me tier up wood , we have accounts of great damage done by the ice in the last freshet all over the country

—8th I piled away the remainder of the wood & cleared up the door[1] some

—9th I hauled up some hemlock logs to door & chopd & split some

—10th I chopd & sp[l]it some for oven wood in fore noon & Niah Hinkley helpd me saw the remainder in afternoon, rather pleasant weather yet.

---

1 TJ used the word "door" to mean "dooryard." (*Cf.* Walt Whitman "When lilacs last in the dooryard bloomed....").

Webster Friday ~~March~~ April 10th 1846

Sally had a very sick night last night & is very feeble to day, more so than she has ever yet been

—11th I split [&] piled away the wood. I went over after Aunt Mariam Hinkley to wait upon Sally. Clarrissa M. went over to Mr. Crowleys about failed us:[?] I painted some of the trimmings on the house in after noon
—1Sun. 12th More cool
—13th I carried Mrs. Hinkley home & painted trimmings & front side of house, very cool & windy
—14th The ground froze very hard last [?] & still cold and windy, I painted the portches , more moderate at night
—15th Thick & snow falling this morning. snow rain & wind by turns through the day, we found early this morning that Sally was failing & I went over after Mrs Hinkley & she continued to fail gradually & at noon could not speak so as to be understood & at half past three P.M. she died—clear & cold at night. Wm. Robinson & Thos. Storer watched at night[1]

—16th Cold this morning but fine & pleasant through the day, I carried Mrs Hinkley home & went over to S. D. Rands to engage him to dig a grave, State Fast[2]

---

1 Although TJ does not use the term "wake" in his journal, friends, neighbors or relatives watched with the deceased until they were buried. Interestingly the English gave up the wake at the time of the Reformation (although it continued to be used by the Irish). The English who settled Maine in the early 17th century would have bypassed the effects of the Reformation and obviously the custom was continued by their descendants—surely a source of comfort for the bereaved. The ritual of watching the dead was a Celtic ritual, one that predated Christianity. (*Encyclopaedia Brittanica*, 11th Ed., NY 1910.)

2 Again, the Fast Day as proclaimed by the governor.

We made preparation for Sallys funeral & the meeting commenced in afternoon, Sermon by Eld[er] Perkins, pleasant afternoon

—18th I went up to W. Spragues in Greene with Ann to see the famous Dr. Mann[1], but he did not arrive till after I left, Saml Robinson & wife , A. Davis & Wife stopd[2] till he arrived, very bad waggoning[3], had a little rain & thunder before I got home

—Sun 18th Smart rain last night & some this morning—Afternoon I and Ann went up to Greenleaf Spoffords to see Dr. Mann, he soon arived & prescribed for Ann, got home about eleven in evening, quite a number present

—20th I went up to Mr. Spoffords to conduct the Dr over to B. Dyers to see his wife, did not get him started till late in afternoon, got over to Mr Dyers the Dr gave encouragement about Mr. Dyer.

—21st I & Reuben Dyer who began work yesterday for half the time this season sawed bunks[4] for fencing in the pasture in fore noon & piled up chips &c in afternoon, very fine & drying

—22d & 23d S. Coursen R. Dyer & I made fence round the plowed piece in the pasture

—24th & 25th at work on fence by Factory road

---

1 I have been unable to identify Dr. Mann. Ann was TJ's and Mary Ann's oldest daughter who was then 14. The journal gives no clue as to what her ailment was.

2 "stopd" = "stayed"

3 TJ's spelling is correct; "wagon" is a later usage.

4 "bunks" were fence-posts.

Webster Sunday April 26th 1846

Windy & very drying, but very cold nights of late I & Mary Ann went over to N. Jordans in afternoon

—27 I nearly completed the fence on factory road Reuben Dyer not helping this week

—28 Finishd fence on factory & set some posts & rails, hauld away banking &c in fore noon & hauld stone off of a piece of ground by what we call the old house workd hard & late missed a yearly heifer at the barn

—29th I rose early searched the pasture for the missing heifer & to [no] effect, but heard of her at J. Blethens last night & followed her by track to Isaac Thompsons & then found her; I harrowed on the pasture ground the remainder of the day.

—30th Dull & rainy the most of the day, I cracked plaster for grinding.

—May 1st I harrowed on pasture ground in fore noon & sowed oats on the same in afternoon came on to rain before night

—2d Quite rainy all day, whet saws for N. Hinkley,

—Sunday 3d Dull, rain & sun shine today

—4th I harrowed in oats

—5th I rolld oat ground

— 6th I went up to the mills in the morning & got buts off wheat ground in fore noon & cultivated & harrowed in afternoon.

—7th Sowd three bushels of wheat, dry & fine for farming

—8th planted potatoes on pasture ground, where the first house on the place stood[1]

---

1 TJ's father, Ephraim Jordan, is said to have built a log cabin on the land shortly after he purchased it in 1788. Possibly the "old house" was that building.

Webster Saturday May 9th 1846

I sowd one bushel wheat bought [from] B. Sandborn some rain in fore noon

—11th I cut potatoes the most of the fore noon & went into the woods & got stuff for seven posts, & hewd & made them in afternoon & hauld them down to the old pasture plowed piece, Mary Ann was up to John Pettingills

—12th I completed fencing the pasture ground, oats are up, cold north west wind

—13th I began to plant potatoes on the piece west of the spring, stormy southerly wind

—14th Planting potatoes again strong southerly wind again seized with a diziness in my head to day.[1]

—15th Finished planting the potatoe piece, mended some fence in the swamp &c very dizy head

—16th Saml. Coursen helpd me, hauling manure & plowed garden

—Sunday 17th I went to meeting serm by J. A. West

—18th R. Dyer helps me the comeing week, hauld manure & got ready & plowed some, put of[f] by some rain

—19th plowed all for corn by Factory road, quite cool.

—20th Finishd plowing in fore noon & harrow'd some, harrowed the remainder in afternoon, some rain

—21st Began to put out manure

—22d put out manure & planted the most of the piece. E. Jordan sent two hands to help me.

---

1 This is the first time that TJ mentions a troubling condition that recurred the following year. It probably was labyrinthitis ("Meniere's disease")—a benign but disabling ailment. It may be associated with middle ear infection but more often the etiology is unknown.

Webster Saturday May 23rd 1846

We planted the remainder of the corner ground & harrowd & put out manure for corn below hard sweet apple trees some little rain at night

—Sun 24th Very fine & warm after the morning, Niah Jordan & wife up part of the day

—25 I planted some corn & beans, some rain

—26th I put out one load of manure & finish'd planting corn & beans except some short rows, some sun in fore noon & dull in afternoon

—27 Went up to Green to carry home E. Barrels buck[1], afternoon wheeled off stones & stuck sticks to string corn, still dull

—28th I made garden

—29th Finish'd garden & went after Dr. for Mary Ann being quite unwell for some ten days past, had Celiann Sawyer since 25th

—30th Yet dull & some wet Eld Seth Stetson stayed with us last night I went up to Mark Lowels in afternoon

—Sunday 31st At home all day dull & stipid [stupid] or I might have gone to meeting although had some rain

——June 1st Planted Beans set some garden fence, made stump fence, & hauld one load of stuff for pickets from the mill, fine & pleasant

—2d 3d 4th & 5th At work on highway very warm & fine

— 6th We had very heavy shower last night, S. Jordan help me wash our sheep early, jobd round the remain'd of day

---

1. TJ apparently borrowed a ram to impregnate his ewes.

Webster June Sun 7th 1846

Clear & pleasant, Mrs Rebecca & Mrs Polly Gould up here

—8th I went to Topsham sold butter for 12 1/2 cents went round Bowdoinham & engaged to carry 12 bushels potatoes for two yards of broadcloth, got home & sowed some barley

—9th I & R. Dyer & E Jordan 2d workd on highway for N. Jordan

—10th I carried 14 1/2 bushels potatoes down to Bowdoinham, got home & done some painting on house trimmings & portch floor

—11 I sheered sheep

—12th I finishd sheering sheep in fore noon & painted on s. end of house in afternoon

—13th I went up to Lewiston early, painted in fore noon after I got home—Afternoon I helpd Joseph Blethen move his barn, I was unwell with a cold

—14th We went to meeting at Four Corners very warm & pleasant & some dry

—15th Began to weed corn, drove twelve sheep & twelve lambs up B. Dyers to pastuere & sold 16 bushel potatoes to Jesse Donnell

—16th & 17 & 18 very fine finished weeding corn

—19th Began to hoe potatoes over in the pasture some rain

—20th Finish'd the pasture potatoes & harrowed potatoes in the field & hoed some.

—21st Somme rain & very cold, I went over to B. Dyers & over to Niah Hinkleys & to Garcelons & got [word unreadable]

Webster Monday June 22d 1846

I went after Dr. Garcelon for Father who has been sick some ten days. I carried wool to Corbets to be carded

—up to 28th I howed potatoes two days, harrow'd corn & potatoes, pulled thistles from wheat, spent two half days in making alterations in Fathers truss[1], went to mill & tended Father &c &c.

—29th Reuben finished hoeing potatoes & finished pulling thistles out of wheat & barley, harrowd corn at night, very warm

—July 1st Hoed the corn by the corner & got wine, Lemons & oranges for Father at Garcelons having sent to Augusta for them.

—2d Rainy in fore noon sprouted potatoes[2], afternoon pealed hemlock bark & piled[3]

—4th I went to Topsham early & got a grindstone, got home shortly after noon, Reuben went home in afternoon, & I hung the grindstone, &c.. very warm day

—Sun. 5th Very warm in fore noon, comes in foggy & some rain late in afternoon

—6th I jobd round house in fore noon & hoed corn in afternoon & went to Factoryville after rolls[4]

—7th & 8th & 9th in fore noon I helpd James Bryint frame a saw mill very warm hoed some in afternoon of 9th

---

1 The only treatment for Ephraim's hernia(s) would have been a truss. Surgery would have been considered only if the hernia became strangulated, a condition that would almost certainly have been fatal, with or without an operation.

2 "brushing off the eyes [of potatoes] if they have a tendency to sprout." Baxter *Libr. Pract. Agric.* ed. 4, 1846, Cited in OED.

3. TJ later takes this bark to South West Bend, presumably to a tannery.

4 TJ mentions "rolls" several times in his diary. He was probably referring to boards with a rounded top used in roofing and elsewhere, *i.e.* "half-round."

Webster Friday July 10th 1846

I finish'd hoeing corn & beans, very warm indeed.

—11th I mended rakes, made a grindstone crank for Wm. Coursen, made three new rakes & went to the Factory Ville after rolls, excessive hot weather

—Sun 12th Warm & fine weather for corn—Father is no better, has taken no food exceept in drink since the eighth, low & feeble

—13th Began to mow, afternoon we cleaned out barn & put cart together, &c.

—14th Dull & some rain in fore noon, at work in garden, afternoon mowed some

—15th 16th & 17th tolerable hay weather

—18th dull & some rain

—Sun 19th Some dull

—20th 21st & 22 decent hay weather

—23rd dull & some rain I shelld corn &c.

—24th Fine in fore noon but rather dull in afternoon

—25th Quite rainy & much needed to

—Sun 26th Dull, Cloudy & not much sun shine—Father remains about the same for two or three weeks past, is got up three times a day & has his bed made, & no more appetite.

—27th 28th & 29th First rate hay weather

—30th Dull we got in one load early, some rain I went over to J. Haskals & got a large pitch fork

Webster July Thurs. 30th 1846

Samuel Donnell come to help me, mowed some in fore noon very worm, mowd & raked some in afternoon, had very fine shower, so as to wet the ground nicely

—31st Dull I mended hay rack, drawed of[f] vinegar, hoopd cider barrel & rake some &c, &c.

—August 1st Pretty fair mow'd by the house & got in three load

—Sun 2d Very fine indeed—Father remains about the same

—3d B. Dyer, S. Donnell, S. and Reuben mowd most of the fore noon below the orchard & got I all in, halld seven load

—4th Mowed a piece of stout grass below the gate and sweet apple tree & mowed some clover—very warm

—5th mowd some & got in six load very warm indeed

—6th We finishd mowing in fore noon & got in one load, very extremely warm, while at dinner some thunder & signs of a shower, we put off one load of hay & got in another in great haste, a showe struck just as we got the barn, had a smart shower & some hail, very severe in some places, had three load out to get wet

—7th tolerable fair, finishd up haying

—8th I went over to four corners & got horse shod at Colbys in fore noon

Afternoon pitched over manure &c had another shower

—Sun 9th I went up to B. Dyers in afternoon. Ebenezer Colby buried yesterday

—10th I went to Factory to mill in fore noon, and pitched over manure remaining part of the day except a shower in afternoon Reuben did not work to day

—11th Mowed three bushels sowing wheat much damaged by wevil and mowd some oats & peas

—12th We mowed some more oats & peas & got in three load wheat. Stephen Day helpd us in afternoon

—13th We pitched off two load of wheat & raked and got in one load & all and pitched wheat off in fore noon E. Jordan 2d helpd us— Afternoon mow'd remainder of oats & peas & raked and got in one load

—14th Dull in fore noon, reap seed hay & got threshing machine ready & threshed the most of the load we got in yesterday

— 16th We finishd threshing the load of oats & reap some wheat of the bushel I bought B Sandford not being injured by wevil turned up oats & got in two load & all

—Sun 16th Warm and pleasant

—17th I & Reuben undertook to get a load of oats out of the barn & put the oxen on the hind part of the load & I took hold of the tounge [tongue] & got thrown down & the tongue [continued on next page]

fell directly upon my breast, bruiseing me severely & dislocating my collar bone, plain enough my work was done for a season, very warm today. Dr. Garcelon sent for at night, very, very lame & sore, Father is so as to set some & has some app5tite

—18th My stomach is dreadfully sore, Reuben & E. Jordan 2d reap & shock'd the wheat, cooler

—19, 20, 21, 22, & Sun 23d Almost entirely helpless, not able to get out of bed[1]

—24th Some better—or beginning to mend, today we have Mr. Dyer Reuben & oxen Ivory Coursen & Jesse Greene here & go up to work on the new County road from Lewiston to Gardiner

—25th & 26th The same crew & about canceled my tax

—27th Quite fair I am mending slowly

—28th Mr. J. Gould & wife up here, I went up to the corn with Mr Gould, Reuben & children diging potatoes down by the old house, very warm

—29th John Davis buried to day of Lewiston—N. Jordan helpd Reuben thresh the remainder of our oats & peas, dull all day. A drover took away two two year old heifers & one pair yearling steers that I sold a few days since for $40.00

—Sun 30th Some rain in the morning, quite warm, John Robinson of St. Albans up & in to see us last evening

—31st Reuben winnowd some oats & peas & pulld beans, dry & warm

---

1 One can only guess what the nature of TJ's injury was, although clearly it was severe. A "dislocated" collar bone might have been a fracture, or possibly a separation of either the acromio-clavicular joint or of sterno-clavicular joint at the ends of the clavicle. None of these injuries alone should have caused so much debility, so he almost surely had other injuries as well—possibly fractured ribs which are notoriously painful, or an intra-abdominal injury of some sort.

Webster Tuesday Sept 1st 1846

Winnowed remainder of oats & peas & pulld beans & hauld down a load to the barn. A man that is about setting aqueduc pumps took dinner with us today

—3d Saml. Coursen threshd out grass seed & some barley &c.

—4th Coursen helpd me again & cut up corn

—5th Very warm indeed

—Sun. 6. I went out in the field & into the corn & Jesse Davis came up & I had a long talk about the suit between Lisbon & Webster in reference to William Davis. Still very warm

—7th Reuben cut stalks & I went to Coombs mill so called to mill, Moodys mill not repaired

—8th I went to four Corners, & picked some seed corn in afternoon, Reuben & children dug potatoes

—9th The new Meeting House in the Clough District dedicated today, E Jordan 2d & Reuben cut stalks in afternoon

—10th E. Jordan 2d Reuben & children dug potatoes in forenoon & Reuben & children finishd the pasture piece in afternoon, E.J. cut up corn

—11th N. J. came & repaired threshing machine & threshed the Sandborn[1] wheat 5 1/9 bush.

—12th Threshed on mowd wheat all day. I forgot to mention that we had some frost on the morning of the 10th

—Sun. 13th Warm & very dry

---

1 TJ had obtained wheat for seeding from B. Sandborn on May 9. 1846.

Webster Sept 14th 1846

I went to annual election. Getting quite smart[1]

—15th we finishd threshing wheat

—16th Winnowed wheat 22 bushels from three bushels of red wheat

—17th Ivory Coursen Silas Jordan &c got wheat straw up in the barn in fore noon & I was up to E. Jordans 2d to help repair threshing machine, & got in some corn in afternoon

—18th & 19th husked out & sorted corn

—Sun 20th At meeting serm by EB Stetson

—21st B. Jordan help us get in corn & husk Some rain

—22d I went over to J. Haskals & got cart tyre set. Reuben & Ivory Coursen dug potatoes

—23d The same crew dug potatoes again & finishd had about 60 bushels

—24th Husked out & sorted corn & cut up some

—25th some rain last night, got in the remainder of the corn by the corner & husked it out

—26th Sorted up the corn huskd yesterday & Reuben went home, some rain

—Sun 27th I went up to Wm Coursens & to E. Jordans 2d to get them to help me get in corn

—28th Got in corn pumpkins & gathered apples, Niah H. came up & carried Mary Ann down. Their mother being very sick at his house

—29th I gathered apples in fore noon & went down & brought Mary Ann home in afternoon, her mother is very sick

—30th I went to the Factory to mill & up to see Mrs Hinkley [continued on next page]

---

1 "smart" = "brisk," evidently referring to seasonal cold.

who is very low indeed. I husked corn the remainder of the day. Mary Ann went down to see her mother & found her dead & from thence to J. Goulds & found their little girl very sick & died about twelve oclock

—Oct. 1st I husked all day

—2d We went down to the Congregational Meeting House to the funeral of Mrs. Hinkley & little Mary Gould, dull day & some rain

—3d I finished husking soon after dinner & went down to help raise the top story of sawmill—I went down to Factory ville after

—Sun 4th I went over to meeting serm by A.J. West

—5th R. Dyer & I sorted corn, had fifty bushels from a piece in the upper field, we had about 140 bushels in all. Mary Ann went down to Capt Davis & sprained her foot, so as to be quite lame Cap. Ds wife had a young son

—6th & 7th Cleared the barn & Gathered apples &c.

—8th Hauled pumpkins in forenoon & we went down to se[e] Mrs. Gould in afternoon

—9th Fenced door yard before wood house, winnowed beans & got in graft apples &c had a little shower

—10th I went down to Factory to mill early cool & windy hauld muck in fore noon & got in timber chips in afternoon

—Sun 11th Pleasant day, hard frost last night. S. Whitney of Lisbon buried today

Webster Monday Oct. 12th 1846

I wheeled wood in wood house & got in some Mangelwortzel[1], S. Storer came up, brought fish & got apples

—13th Storer went home, came on to rain in afternoon with a severe S. E. gale in the evening

—14th I repaird waggon &c

—15th I got horse shod & went to mill in fore noon & killd some mutton & got ready to go to Bath in afternoon

—16th I went to Bath & got home about nine oclock in evening

—17th I got in carrots & went to mill at Factory Ville in afternoon

—Sun 18 dull & rain & some snow in afternoon

—19th Hauld manure

—20th Plow'd stubble land in at pasture

— 21st & 22d Reuben D. helpd Mr Robinsons plow with our team, & I shoveled up some manure got in turnips & got plow sharpened & ironed on 21st & cleard out the little house & got in wood on 22d some rain at night

—23d Hauld manure again.

—24th Plowd stubble land in fore noon & helpd to set off widow Mary Jordans dower[2] in C. Mars[?] form in afternoon with Jesse Davis & James Bryant set off three acres of improved land & ten acres & 9 rods of unimproved land & one front room & the N.E. corner of the barn

—Sun 25 Cool & raw, fall like

---

1 "mangel-wortzel" a large-rooted variety of beet used as cattle fodder.

2 The dower was that part of a deceased husband's or wife's estate which the law allowed to the widow or widower for life. Eessentially it was the survivor's legal right to real-estate, or the income therefrom, usually one third, for the remainder of the survivor's life. "C. Mars form" is what TJ wrote but clearly he meant "farm."

Webster Monday Oct 26th 1846

I went to the mill in fore noon & spread manure in afternoon Mary Ann went down to Niahs[1] his child being quite sick

—27th Wm. Robinson & Joseph Pray helpd me plow sward land, I changed oxen with Wm Crowley

—28th Rainy

—29th Plowed again, fine day

—30th Samuel Coursen helpd me plow & finish stubble land, very cold & snowy all day

—31st We got apples in the cellar, rather cold

—Sun Nov. 1st went to meeting at four Corners serm. by A.J. West

—2d I made ready to go to Bath

—3d I went to Bath some rain going & comeing & very mudy—Niah Hinkleys child buried today, died yesterday morning

—4th I cut out & partly closed myself a pair of boots, some rain in morning

—5th made one boot

—6th & 7th In fore noon I helpd Mr. Robinson plow very warm & fine—afternoon of 7th I finished my boots

—8th Sun Very pleasant , I went over to N. J.s the first time since last June

—9th I went to Factory Ville to mill & got dressed cloth[2] & necklace for Mary Ann that Mr. Gerrish got for her. I hauled manure, dirt &c.

—10th I helpd M. Robinsons plow in fore noon & mended shoes in afternoon

—11th I made Ann a pr of shoes

—12th I went up to help J. Cushing raise a mill, cold & raw N.E. wind

—13th We went up to J. Davis in fore noon & helpd Cushing raise his mill in afternoon, cool but pleasant.

---

1 Niah Hinkley was MaryAnn's brother, the child was her nephew.

2 "dressed cloth" probably meant decorated or printed cloth.

Webster Saturday Nov 14th 1846

I split some stone to make fence by the springs

—15th Sun. I went to meeting serm. by J. C. Knowlton rather able discourse I thought

—16th I got our stone for more fence by the springs, over by N. Jordans raw N.E. Wind in fore noon, more pleasant in afternoon

—17th E. Jordan 2d help'd me haul together & block up the stone spoken of yesterday, to haul in the winter quite pleasant

—18th I hooped barrels &c

—19th I wheeled door dung & hauled hog manure, some rain in evening, I worked late repairing takle blocks[1]

—20th Niah Hinkley & Samuel Coursen help'd me butcher two hogs weighing 500 lb & 390 lb

—21st I cut up & salted pork & ground one load of apples for cider very windy & cold last night, but more moderate today

—Sun. 22d Mary Ann, Ann & Elizabeth went to meeting at the new Meeting House near A. Boubiers in Lewiston

—23d I made cider, some rain in morning but comes off clear & cold G. Pullen of Augusta came in at evening & stop'd with us

—24th Very cool I got home cider hauld some dirt &c in fore noon & hauld some stone together in afternoon by N. Jordans

—25th I whet cross cut saw in fore noon & saw'd some lumber logs in afternoon

---

1 "takle" (tackle) meant rope and a "block" was a pulley. "Takle blocks" in this instance probably meant simply pulleys, presumably to be used for moving stone.

came on to snow just as night [fell]

—26th Very high wind last nigh[t]. The snow is all in heaps & no sleighing I made Rowena a pair of shoes

—27th I cut & closed a pair of thin shoes for Drusilla Dyer in fore noon & went to factory Ville in afternoon after sole leather

—28th Another small snowtorm. I made the shoes I began yesterday

—Sun 29th Very moderate, I went up to B. Dyers in afternoon

—30th S. Clausen helpd me chop in the woods, cool & windy

—Dec 1st & 2d Chopd in the wood

—3d Anual Thanksgiving killd a beef cow

—4th chopd wood again

—5th I made Martha a pair of shoes

—6th Sun. clear & cool Father went to the door & slip'd down, rather lame at Supper time[1]

—7th Chop'd wood in the woods, David Sanborn stayed with us. Father did not take breakfast with us more feeble than usual, but was about house & to the door in the course of the day

—8th Stormy snow first & then rain. I whet N. Jordans wood saw &c Father was very feeble or stupid, took some breakfast & was not up for the day & did not say anything after & was not up after laying down in the fore noon

---

1. TJ has mentioned his father, Ephraim Jordan (1764-1846), several times in the journal. He would have been about 82 years old. He was doing well in the spring when TJ made him new shoes, then became sick in July—TJ worked on his truss then. He appears to have recovered, but from this day's episode he went downhill. He died on December 11th. 1846.

Webster Wed Dec 9th 1846

Father is very feeble does not speak at all & takes no food. Mrs Davis & Mrs Pettengill are with us

—10th Father remains in about the same stupid state, but is more feelbl [sic]

—11th Fails gradually & died about three Oclock in the afternoon, some snow in the night & this morning—J. Blethen & N. Jordan came in to set up for the night, very windy

—12th we was alone the most of the day, cold & windy

—Sun 13th E. Jordan 2d & Stephen Day was her[e] last night, funeral commenced at ten oclock. AM, Severe cold & and windy when we went to the grave—Sermon by A.J. West from Job 14c. & 14th verse

—14th I layed some beding under three year old steer & chored round the house

—15th I made Holmon a pr of shoes very windy

—16th I went to Topsham with butter to H. Perkins, sold for one shilling in cash, tolerable pleasant

—17th & 18th I shelled some corn—Hannah Weymouth here & partly made me a large jacket & I carried her home to Wm. Moodys, very cold & commenced snowing in the morning of 18th

—19th Mrs Robinson finishd my jacket, snowed again

—Sun 20th We went up to new Meeting House to meeting, Mr. Miller Preacher

20th Began to keep P Colbys cow by the week.

Webster Mon. Dec 21st 1846

I went to Topsham & carried eight bushels corn & got iron to iron a pung bottom, tolerable sleighing

—22d 23d 24th I 25th I hauld out some logs &c.

—26 I chop'd some wood at the door in fore noon, very windy& a little snow that fell last night flew merrily, I went to Factory & carried soap to Corbet

—27 we went over to Meeting—I forgot Mention that we was up to B. Dyers on a visit on the even. of 24th

—28th I killd two pigs Saml Coursen helpd me, very fine & pleasant

—29th I started early for market very cold & windy. I went to Bath & sold my pigs weighing 237 lb each for 5 3/4 cents per lb & 70 lb lard for ten cents per lb & got home about 5 oclock in evening

—30th Quite a snow storm

—31st I went into the woods in fore noon & hauld S. Coursen a load of wood in afternoon, moderate & snow giving = January 1st 1847 = I got oxenshod at E. Colbys sitll moderate

—2d I went over to Meeting house to a Society meeting & Mary Mary Ann [sic] went down on the ridge, Niah Hinkley up & I tapd a pr of shoes for him in evening

Sun 3d We went up to new meeting house again to meeting, Mr. Millers farewell sermon

Webster Mon. January 4th 1847

I began to haul wood S. Coursen helping

—Rufus, Joseph & Mary Davis made us an evening visit, snow at night
—5th Rained this morning, we made sassagess [sic] &c
6th very pleasant, hauld wood & Mary Ann went to Little river ville in afternoon
—7th Hauld wood in fore noon & rainy in afternoon, I finished Ezekiel Jones hand sled
—8th hauld wood, clear cold & windy, the swamp is some overflowed & som[e] slippery in open land.
Quite likely to be a cold night
At ten oclock, when I write[1]

—9th I went to mill in fore noon & went up to I. Farris to get some boards to make a pung top & carried wood over to the meeting house in the evening
—Sun 10th We went over to meeting, but had none Mr West being to unwell to attend, afternoon Mary Ann & two girls went up to the new meeting hous; dull and signs of a storm
—11th I got steers shod in fore noon & hauld on load of wood. N.B. Jordan's son Abner here to dinner, hauld wood in afternoon, some snow in fore noon
—12th 13th 14th & 15th hauld wood
— 16th We hauld three load from this side of the swamp in fore noon & about the last, afternoon hauld out a dry load for Mr. Coursen warm & snow quite soft

---

1 TJ recognized the rhyme, for the page is formatted so.

Webster Mon. Jan. 18th 1847

I hauld a load of wood up to S. Coursen early & hauld out logs after, some snow & quite cold,

—19th I hauld logs again & split an ox yoke

—20th & 21st Got a stick & made an ox yoke quite cool weather

—22 I went into the woods & got hard wood, very cold afternoon went in and got a load of hemlock tops , & cut our off ox and slipd off a dew claw[1]

—23d I hauld three load of stone in forenoon for fence by the springs Mr. Pettingill & wife here did not haul stone in afternoon

—Sun 24th I went over to meeting

—25th I hauld stone again

—26th I hauld stone again, & all of the first lot, quite a smart snow storm

—27th Very cold & snow some drifted &c. I went over to S. West Bend to make a market for some bark

— 28th Extremely cold last night I shelld corn today

—29th I made preparation & loaded bark in afternoon

—30th A very severe snow storm last night & today, I whet saws &c

—Sun 31st At work on the road all day & cot one of our steers very bad,

—February 1st I carried children to school I went to mill, chopd wood &c

—2d made Elizabeth a pair of shoes, J. Merrill brought over stuff to make a pair of wheels, B. Dyer is to make them

---

1 The "dew-claw" is a false hoof on the back of the forefoot, It is prominent on canids, but it is present on ungulates, too. It does not touch the ground. Whether this was an accident, or an elective procedure is unclear. As noted earlier, the "off ox" would be on the side away from the driver. An older meaning of "slip" is "remove, something easily."

Webster Wednesday Feb. 3d 1847

I and B. Dyer at work getting out spokes for J. Merrills wheels

—4th set the spokes &c & B. Dyer went home

—5th I was at work all day on said wheels B. Dyer did not come over

—6th I went to mill, made an ax handle & chopd green wood for ashes, quite pleasant.

—Sun 7th I went over to meeting, rather a thin meeting, but I was well paid for going, very remarkable pleasant On 3d we had quite a rain & high wind in evening—all slosh[1] on 4th

—8th Quite snowy in fore noon shelld some corn in fore noon. B. Dyer came over & we commenced work on J. Merrills wheels in afternoon

—9th & 10th At work on & finish'd wheels, very moderate

—11th We got out stuff [f]or riming for a pr of wheels

—12th B. Dyer helpd me saw hemlock logs

—13th I went to the S.W. Bend with a load of bark, cooler

—Sun 14th Cool & clear Nathan B. Jordan of New Portland stayed here last night

—16th I went to S.W. Bend with bark, very cool, Wm. Robinson went with me

—17th B. Dyer & I got out a set of cart cunts [sic][2] for W. Jordan, very cold and windy & snow flies merrily I went to mill at night

—18th I went to Bath, cool morning but pleasant day

—19th & 20th I hauld hemlock logs to the mill

---

1 "slosh" is a correct alternate spelling of "slush"

2 TJ unequivocally wrote "cunts," an English word with only one meaning that has been in common use for nearly a millenium. The word that he meant was "cant," a part of a wheel rim and I suspect that his spelling was an accepted variation of that word. The word is related to the Latin "canthus" a word that meant "tire" (or "felloe"). The tire (or tyre) was an iron hoop of iron that went around a wheel and only later did it come to refer to a rubber tire. The word "felloe" is defined, in turn, as "the curved pieces of wood which, joined together, form the circular rim of a wheel." (OED) All of these terms would be well known to a wheelwright—one of TJ's many skills.

Webster Sunday February 21st 1847

I did not go to meeting because it was cold & dull

—22d I whet A Stanfords wood saw in fore noon & help Jesse Davis get out cart cunts in afternoon

—23 I made ready & started for Portland in afternoon, & very cold too stayed at night at Thaniel Jordans in N. Yarmouth

—24th I went to Portland, sold dried apple for 4 cent per lb meal for 87 cents per bushel & oates for 45 cent & bought 364 lb of iron for 2cts per lb & got back to N. Yarmouth upper corner & stopd at night

—25th I came home after taking five bushels plaster & got S. D. Rand to haul up a barrel molasses from the S.W. Bend

—26th S.D.R. gelded a pig & I chopd wood &c.

—27th I whet S. Coursen's wood saw, quite a damp snow.

—28th We broke out the roads quite a heavy snow & damp

—March 1st I went to N. Yarmouth, carried 8 bushels potatoes & got 8 bushels of plaster, very poor sleighing, a strong crust

—2d We got out hams for bacon &c

—3rd I carried Mary Ann down to E. Jordans & came home & went to mill & went down after Mary Ann, pleasant

4th At work in the shaping a Division door in tyup & went up to Joseph Blethens on a visit

—5th We went down to see Aunt Ham who is quite sick

and calld to Mr. Goulds & to see Mr. Aaron Hinkley who is very sick

—6th At work on a corn sheller

Sun 7th We went to meeting, dull in afternoon

—8th I helpd Niah Hinkley grind an ax in the morning I then went over to the hill by N Js & got one load of stone in fore noon, quite warm & the snow soft; afternoon I finshd the corn sheller & went over & got on a load of stone & got down into the wood & the oxen broke their yoke & I took them of & left the load, the snow has settled very much today

—9th I haulld more stone & all, much colder

—10th We went of over to the Congregational meeting house to the funeral of Uncle Aaron Hinkley, serm by Eld. Fisk, very cold & windy

—11th I went down to Little river to Davis with bacon, three hams weighing 104 lbs at 9 cts per pound half cash, very windy, brought Priscilla Ham home to make some dresses

—12 th Saml Coursen helpd me cut pine tree & haul out for shingle stuff, & hauld out some poles &c very cold & windy

—13th Saml. Coursen chopd wood in fore noon & we sawd shingle bolts. Elizabet carried Miss Ham home, still cold & windy

—Sun 14th We went overto the funeral Aunt Anna Hinkley, serm by Mr. Fisk a[t] his M [eeting] house

Webster Monday March 15th 1847

I went to anual town meeting, P.M. Garcelon, Wentworth Jordan &
James Ham chosen Selectmen, Assessors and overseers of poor,
Melvin Henderson chosen Collector Treasurer & Constable, raised
$425 for town expenses, $450 for schools, & $100 to finish the new
road & 150 dollars to build a town house, voted to build a town house
& chose a Committee draught a plan of the same & receive proposals
for building. S. Jordan, Jesse Davis & Thomas Henderson being said
committee. We stopd at Hugh Weymouth's house to decide on the size
form &c.

—16th I went over to the Clerks to see the record, wrote of a plan or
two & went over to the four Corners to finish them got home about
eleven of the clock A.M.

—17th I went up to the mills to put up a notice in fore noon & up to
Lewiston, to engage[1] or partially engage some gravestone & went up
to B Dyers on my way home, to have him come down to help me on W.
Jordans's wheels

—18th We went up to Went. Jordan's on a visit, rath[er] more moderate

—19th Very pleasant We went up to Mr. Robinsons in evening & was
sent for Holmon being sick

—20th Wentworth Jordan & H. Polly chopd wood at the door, & I
went over to four corners to receive proposals for building town house

---

1 TJ often speaks of engaging various services or items, either ones that he intends to
supply or will obtain from others. At that time the word "engage" had the meaning of
"contracting for," or "agreeing to provide in the future."

Rather dull B. Dyer & J. Hodgskins came over here B. Dyer wishing to get released for two days, John Woodbury called to see us, Mr. Titcomb here—Rebecca Dyer is quite sick

=[1] I pild away the wood &c

23d I went to mill in fore noon, & at work making a drag the rest of the day N. Jordan & wife here in afternoon

=B. Dyer & I was at work on N. Jordans cart spokes & cart for J. L. Davis, B. Dyer went home & Mary Ann was soon sent for to go & watch with Rebecca Dyer being very sick

26the I got out J. Davis cart spokes

=27th I drove the spokes in N. Jordans cart hubs.

=28th We went up to B. Dyers Rebecca was very sick indeed

=29th I went down to the mill & took a bond of John Bryen for building a own house in company with Jesse Davis, at work on N.Js wheels the remainder of the day

=30th & 31st at work on sd wheels, Ann & Elizabeth went up to B. Dyers to see how Rebecca was & soon returned with the news that she was dead

=April 1st We went up to B. Dyers in fore noon, at work on the wheels in afternoon

=2d We went up to the funeral of Rebecca Dyer Discourse by Mr French, very stormy all day

=3d I finished N, Js wheels & carried hem up to him, quite thawy today

=Sun. 4th I went to meeting paid $250 to A. J. West

---

1 For this and several subsequent pages for some reason TJ doubled or tripled the dashes he used in separating his entries, represented here with an equal sign.

Webster Monday April 5th 1847

I went down & hauld two load of wood for Mr. Spears B. Dyer came & we went to work on spoke & cunts for a pair of wheels for S. Davis

= 6th We got ready & began to drive the first spoke in J.S. Davis hubs & broke the hub=did not do much in afternoon

—7th We got Mr. Marrs hubs, we drove three or four spokes & broke one of them hubs—then I weighed B. Dyer a ton of hay, rather thawy for a day or two past

=8th & 9th We made Mr. Marrs wheels

=10th We undertook to drive another spoke in J.S. Davis hubs & broke out another, I went down to see him & he gave up the idea of having a new pair & sent up an old wheel to repair & we went to work & nearly finishd it, this job & three days work on Wentworth & Davis wheels, Dyer is to ofset against my work on J. Merrills wheels, & I paid him three dollars for his part of Mr. Marrs wheels

=Sun 11th Very cold & windy all day

=12th Saml. Coursen helpd me chop wood

=13th S. Coursen helpd me chop again, I boiled cart fellows[2]

—14th I helpd E. Jordan 2d frame a barn

=15th I went up to E Jordan2d came on to rain, came home & tap'd shoes &c

16th I help E. Jordan 2d finish framing his barn & S Coursen helpd him for me, very cold & froze hard last [night?]

(

Wednesday April Sat. 17th 1847

Snow & rain in fore noon. I whet saws &c & went over to Henry
Carvill to select a place to set a town hous[e] in company with Jesse
Davis & Thomas Henderson

—Sun 18th I went to meeting at four Corners very cold indeed &
windy too
=19th I went down to Little River & call to see Priscilla Ham to
engage her to keep our school but she could not engage. The ground
froze uncommon hard for the season this morning=E. Jordan 2d helpd
me chop wood
=20th E. Jordan 2d help'd me chop & S. Coursen helpd me saw shingle
stuff
=21st stormy whet N Js saw, shelld corn &c
=22 E Jordan 2d helpd me finish choping wood=rather pleasant
=23 Another snow storm, shelld corn, tapd my boots &c
=24th put wood in wood house & tierd[1] up out door, tolerable pleasant

Sun 25th We went to meeting at the F[?] W. house raw southerly wind
Eld Lamb preached

=26th George Jordan son of Timothy J. came down a week ago to day
to commence work for the season
26th [sic] pilld up all the wood, took away house banking & split up
some oven wood, dull & aw wind all day.
—27th Some rain in forenoon & very cold in afternoon. We sawd
some logs &c
28th Uncommon cold & freezing last night, & cold to day

---

1 The verb "to tier" means to pile in tiers. It also can be an alternate spelling of the word
"to teer," a word that means "to spread or cover with earth. . . .[or] . . . . to daub with clay"
OED .The first meaning appears to be operative here, as TJ has cut wood that needed to
be piled up.

I hauld stone posts up to the house from the Factory road, I went in to see William Wentworth who is very very low & feeble

—29th We had several inches of snow last night, I went up to S. Coursens in a sleigh , & people were sleding, S. Coursen help me saw up & split a large hemlock log at the door in fore noon & rainy in afternoon

—30th I went over to help N. Jordan make a wood sled

May first at work for N. Jordan—I forgot to mention that in the evening of 29th Mrs Wentworth send up for me to go down Mr. Wentworth being more unwell, I went down & found him very ill stayed late & R. Dyer being at our house, went in & stayed all night, I went in on morning of 30th still feeble, went in at night again.

May 1st I went in , in the morning & he told me he did not rest any last night, soon after I got home from N.Js Mrs. Wentworth sent for me again. I went & found him very low & failing, & died just before seven oclock, I shaved him & assisted in laying him out &c

=Sun 2d I went to Topsham & Brunswick after Mrs Ws. three daughters, got home about noon, tolerable pleasant in fore noon, but some rain in afternoon

=3d Some snow this morning I prepared the schoolhouse for the funeral of Mr Wentworth & attend in afternoon, being quite pleasant

Webster Tuesday May 4th 1847

I hewed some timber for gates & went up to Mr. Pettengills & J. Carvills to find a school Mistress, & went over to four Corners & pulld corn buts &c. toleable [sic] pleasant.

=5th Hauld off stone & harrowd some broke up ground for potatoes in fore noon & picked stones in afternoon.

=6th I went over to Dr. Garcelon's in fore noon to get scions[1], Mr. Bachelder being here grafting. I hauld down shingle butts & harrowd some in afternoon very fine

=7th I harrowd in fore noon & beat the dirt out of corn buts & hauld off some

=8th Hauld off corn buts & cultivated for wheat some rain by spells
=Sun. 9th very fine again
=10th Warm and drying, we harrowd wheat ground & sowd one bushel of English wheat.
—11th Sowd three bushels of wheat & harrowd & rolld it all. Enoch Hinkley came up, having just got home from Virginia

—12th Harrowd on the pasture field
—13th Sowd oates on this pasture ground & harrowd them in: Old Mr. Andrews Boubier buried to day, cooler to day
=14th Rolld the above ground in fore noon & planted potatoes in afternoon, quite unwell this morning
= I sowd some onion seed planted potatoes in the garden.
Sun. 16th Very fine indeed, did not got to meeting not well & some lazy
—17th I got three pigs of John Carvill for which I paid 5 dollars and 50 cent, S. Coursen help me haul manure fine day
—18th quite rainy the first this spring of any amount

---

* Refers to small branches of fruit trees to be used for grafting onto another tree.

Webster Wednesday May 19th 1847

I and George [Jordan] plowd some for corn, dull to day

=20th S. Coursen helpd me plow & finish a piece directly west of the spring

—21st I Harrowd on broke up ground for corn in fore noon & George planted potaoes & I harrowd the old ground with mare & steers & George cross harrowd broke up ground & rolld old ground in afternoon

—I and George put in manure in fore noon very cold & raw, & raind some in afternoon, I mended some fence in the woods

Sun 23d pleasant

=24th S. Coursen helpd me put out manure & plant corn, dull & some rain

—25th quite rainy chored round hous

26th Dull got smith work done &c in fore noon & put out dung in afternoon

=27th S. Coursen helpd us plant again.

=28th Very fine, finishd planting corn & put out some manure for potatoes, rained before night

=30th I went to meeting at four Corners serm by Mr. West,. I saw at meeting Benjamin Pettengill of New York whom I had not seen for many years

—31st we about finish'd planting potatoes planted beans.

June 1st Very rainy in fore noon. I oiled harness, afternoon not much rain & I jobd round, ground broad ax hewd gate post &c.

—2d We cleard off a piece of ground in the pasture in fore noon & William Robinson helpd me plow it in afternoon, quite fine

Webster Sunday June 3 1847

I went to Topsham, very fine indeed, sold butter for 18c per lb & ??ed [cored?] apple sliced for 8c & quartered for 6c, at work in the garden after I got home

—4th Very rainy in fore noon put yarn[1] on the corn ground & shelld corn in fore noon & got work done at Colby's in afternoon

—5th S. Coursen help'd me commence the new fence between field & pasture by the springs, rather cool wind in afternoon.

Sun. 6th Quite cool S.W. wind

—7th S. Coursen helpd me again, laid all the stone & drilld them all

—8th I got rods for the whole & put on rails & pickets on quite a piece[2]

—9th put on rails and pickets till prevented by rain in afternoon I made some posts after quite rainy

—10th finishd the fence in fore noon, hauld two load of rails & pickets from the mill early this morning, afternoon fenced the piece of pasture ground

—11th We washed sheep planted beans on the pasture piece below the orchard spaded up pig yard & planted cucumbers &c and went to the S. W. Bend in afternoon & bought a fire frame[3], pans &c. sold oats for 60 cents per bushel, smart S. wind & quite a rain at night

—12th I got out some potatoes & started about 11 in fore noon for Bowdoinham & got down in Bowdoin & heard that potatoes were low & turned about & went to Littleriverville, & sold to Davis for 45 cents per bushel

---

1 "yarn" is correct, but what TJ meant is unclear.

2 It is not clear how TJ's fence was made. apparently it was a picket fence with stone fence posts often used in New England. The "rods" apparently connected the posts and the pickets would have been nailed to the rods.

2 An iron frame that demarcated the opening to a fireplace around which masonry was laid.

Webster Sunday June 13 1847

Very fine indeed I did not go to meeting, feeling rather poor excuse by the way & Mr. Spears having the promise of the horse to attend the funeral of Aaron Nutting who died on the evening of 10th

= 14th Some rain in the morning, dull all day Jesse Davis, David Davis of Lewiston having been apointed by Judge of Probate to divide & set off the real Estate of Andrew Boubier late of Lewiston to the heirs, commenced that duty this morning, took dinner a[t] Amos Davis's

—15th Began upon the task, again, having surveyed yesterday, viewed this for noon for the purpose of making equal division, took dinner at A Davis again, rainy in afternoon, computing the quantity & location to be assigned to the several heirs

—16th Set off an[d] assigned the home stead to he heirs in six lots, and made returns to Probate office

—17th At work on highway quite fine

=18th Sheared sheep, very fine indeed

—19th I was at on the bridge putting on railing in fore noon & harrwd corn & potatoes in afternoon strong W. wind in afternoon

—20th rainy all day

—21st I started early in the morning & went to Winthrop Ville. To get Counsel of Seth May concerning the town house being built by P. Johnson I saw said May & he told me that Johnson could not recover pay of the town. Rainy in fore noon, but very rainy in afternoon the ground is unually wet.

22d I went down to Mr. Davis in forenoon & down to the mill & I made a request to call a town meeting

Webster June 22d 1847

Afternoon I went over to Mr Hendersons to get signers to a request to call a town meeting, I went round by W. Jordans and home, quite rainy again in afternoon

233d Dull in the morning but clears off in fore noon, W. Jordan calld & took the request to make a warrant, I was at work on a gate & gate post in the fore noon & a short time in afternoon, & then went down to Thomas Atwoods to get him to set a fire frame tomorrow & calld at J. Durgin's and got one hundred & fifty brick, & went up J. Blethens to get him to put on some paper on N.W. front room

—24th Mr. Blethens came in the morning to put on paper, & Atwood came in afternoon, he set the fire frame & Blethen put on the paper & I white washed plastering &c.

—25th I wed[1] corn being the first except what George wed yesterday in afternoon—very fine & warm yesterday & to day, much more so than yet

26th very warm indeed, corn weather in earnest, wed[1] corn in fore noon & helpd John Bryant raise an addition to his barn in afternoon, very warm day & night

Sun 27th extremely warm, I did not go to meeting, Niah H. wife & Ophelia came up last night & here all day to day

28th I started early & went to Winthrop again to see S. May & to know if it would be necessary for him to come down to the meeting to be held on the 2d of July next, he thought unnecessary

---

1 TJ's meaning is clear and his usage is correct. The OED notes that "wed" is occasionally used as the past participle of the verb "weed." Since he uses it here consistently, it appears that it was in use in that time and place probably as a holdover from the English spoken by his forebears, as with many other words that TJ uses. "Wed" for "weeded" makes sense when compared with the past participles of "bleed" and "feed."

Webster Monday June 28th 1847

I got home at noon & hoed corn in afternoon

—29th Dull with some rain I made a gate at the passage by the end of the portch &c

30th Still dull in fore noon, I hung & set up a gate at the most westerly pass into the field on the road & cultivated & harrowd the potatoes nearby in afternoon, fine in afternoon

—July 1st Wed corn after the dew was off & potatoes before

—2d. hoed potatoes untill the dew was off & corn after & finished corn in fore noon & I went to the town meeting before spoken of in afternoon, on the first article in the warrant the town voted & chose T. Jordan, Jessie Davis & Thomas Henderson a Committee to purchase land to set the town house upon, contracted for by the building committee, on the second article voted to receive Jonathan Davis at his own offer as sponser for all cost or expense that might arise through Johnson's pretended right to build a town house, fine & pleasant

—3d Hoed potatoes all day & finish'd the piece between the two upper gates, very fine & growing time, corn looks well but small, grain & potatoes look promising

—Sun. 4th Very fine, not at meeting again

5th I went down to the mill after fence palings & hoed beans after, George went home on the night of 3d

=6th hoeing potatoes in the old pasture, they look well

Webster Tuesday July 6th 1847

While hoeing potatoes D.S. Weymouth came into the field & told me that yesterday James Bryant proposed to P Johnson that if he would take John Bs timber for a town house that the said John would take his frame & pay Johnson the difference provided the committee would accept his frame now standing on H Carvills land, to which he replied with an oath that he would let his frame rot where it was before he would do it, Weymouth told me that this morning Johnson came to James B. & said that he would take the timber & leave it to Samson Colby to say what the difference should be, I then told Weymouth I would go over and see the frame that afternoon. I went down to Capt. Davis' & to see Mr. Bryant & found he had not made the agreement in writing & so I came home & harrowd potatoes

=7th I went up to John Carvills to help him on a pair of wheels in fore noon & went over to Mr. Hendersons with Capt. Davis & over to the frame that Johnson put up & concluded that it might answer although it was not according to the plan of the committee[1]

—8th Hoed potatoes George Merrill helping for J. Carvill & finishd those in the pasture, very warm indeed about this time

—9th At work in the garden & fixing up rakes &c

---

1 It is difficult to make sense of all this, but apparently P. Johnson believed that it was his right to build a new town hall and started work on one. This seems not to have been in accord with the community's wishes. To solve the impasse, the selectmen agreed —if the frame that Johnson had erected was suitable—to give him timber and some cash to boot, and use the frame for the new town hall. Johnson initially refused the offer, but then, on the following day, agreed to it.

Webster Saturday July 10th 1847

We put carts together after hauling up some muck helpd Mr. Walton raise a house on the Miller farm & went over to four Corners

—Sun 11th I went to meeting serm by a Mr. Osgood of Auburn

—12th Dull in fore noon began to mow in afternoon

—13th Dull in the morning I pulld thistles out of wheat, in fore noon, some thunder: I changed horses with Warren[1], had a shower in after-noon, & moderate rain the most the afternoon

—14th tolerable hay day raked up what hay we had down into winrow

—15th 16th & 17th R. helpd us

—Sun. 18 Dull with some rain in fore noon

—19th 'We got in some hay & did not mow any being dull in fore noon. Thinning out stuff in garden &c.

—10th Mowd all the fore noon[2], very warm indeed, raked in afternoon

—21st Very warm indeed mowed part of the forenoon, & got in hay, unusual warm last night,

22d & 23d Mowd swamp hay

—24th E. Jordan 2d helped us, fine day & warm in fore noon

=Sun 25th went to meeting Serm by Eld. Stetson, went over to N. Js to see Hannah who is quite sick, some little rain just as [sic] night

—26th Mowd in fore noon & spread out some hay, came up a shower & caught us soon after dinner, then mowd in afternoon

—27th Mowd thin grass in the S.E. corner & got in hay

—28th Mowed in eastern field. Had some rain or sprinkle in afternoon

---

1 TJ's horse trade with Warren will have future repercussions.

2 Mowing machines were not then in common use although a practical mowing machine had just been patented (1844). TJ was still mowing by hand using a long-bladed scythe. Later on, however, he made use of a mowing machine.

Webster Thursday July 29th 1847

Mowd again in eastern field in forenoon & got in that we mowed yesterday & part that we mow'd today

—39th Samuel Donnell helpd us, we mowd all in eastern field & quite a piece in the N.W. corner of the upper field, we got in one load from eastern field that we mowd & one that was mowd before & after supper went up and got Mr Robinson's horse rake raked up & got in two load & all of the piece mowed in fore noon in NW. corner of upper field, some appearance of rain, & much needed being very dry

—31st Began to rain early this morning & rains smartly all the fore noon, & very acceptable

Sun. August 1st Pleasant

—Dull in fore noon, at work in garden, mow'd in afternoon

—3d S. Donnell & B. Whitham help'd us, fine hay day, had Mr Rs. Horse rake again, done fine business

—Had same help again

—4th Had same help again

_5th Had Reuben Dyer & N. J. & Silas came over & help'd us finish mowing & S. Donnell came in afternoon & we got it all in & glad to finish for there is some signs rain

—6th quite cool N.E. wind in in fore noon, more pleasant in afternoon I went to mill & got horse shod &c.

—7th Got up early to go to Yarmouth after plaster but there was great appearance of a storm & so did not go, repaird some fence in fore noon, & pitched over some manure, afternoon very rainy I mended some harness, shoes &c.

Sun 8th Still rainy all day

Webster Monday August 9th 1847

Quite rainy again today. The ground has a fine wetting by this time. I made Mary Ann a pair of thin shoes today

—10th I cut out a pair of shoes for Elizabeth, pitched over manure in he yard, very warm & fine

—11th I went to Yarmouth & got nine bushels plaster, very warm day, Lots of hay to cut in Yarmouth yet.

—12th Sow'd plaster[1] & mowed oats & reap seed hay &c

—13th sow'd more plaster & raked oats I got in one load

—14th Got the machine ready & broke in the horse & threshed the most of the load of oats I go two load more

—Sun 15th pleasant & fine growing weather. The grasshopers and caterpillars are very plenty Some lame in my back or shoulders

—16th I went over to S. Hendersons early after the threshing machine. Very lame, so bad that I could not do any thing, George mowed some wheat

—17th Some rain, did not get in any wheat, but finishd threshing oats
18th got in wheat or winnowd oats & got in wheat
19th threshed some wheat
20th & 21st Saml. Coursen helpd us, we threshed wheat so as to get in the last, I went over to view the town house in fore noon of 21st fine weather.

—Sun. 22d went to meeting at four Corners. Serm. by A.J. West. I went over to B. Dyers & to V. Foss.
23d Finish'd threshing wheat, that is what grew east of the house & mowd a bushel sowing in upper field

---

1 Plaster of Paris (anhydrous calcium sulfate, or gypsum) was used as a top dressing for gardens, effectively increasing crop yield.

Webster August Thursday 24th 1847

We winnowed twelve bushels wheat & got in the wheat mower yesterday, & went over to N. Jordans with oxen & met R. Dyer there & we hauld home the stump machine.

26th Commenced hauling stumps N. Jordan, Varramus [?] Fast, R. Dyer and Oxen helping, fine day & good luck.
27th I helpd S, Jordan split stone Henry Jordan helping some more rain.
—28th I helped D [?] L. Weymouth on the town house, some rain again.
—Sun. 29th Dull in forenoon but pleasant in afternoon, Ann & Elisabeth went down to the Jacob Goulds in afternoon,. George cut some stalks last week
—30th We pulld beans all day, fine
—31st began to thresh the English wheat
—Sept. 1 I Repaird the machine some & threshed the remainder of the wheat in forenoon & pulled beans in afternoon
2d Put up beans to dry
—3d & 4th cut stalks, foggy nights & mornings,
5th Went to meeting serm by Eld Knapp of Litchfield, Pleasant I pulled peas out of potatoes in forenoon, Eld Knapp here at dinner I bought two books of him, afternoon about six of the clock we had the adddition of a fine boy baby[1] to our family, I have a bad cold at this time.

—7th I went after Rebecca Gould to take care of Mary-Ann

---

1 Albert was the last of TJ and Mary Ann's children and their second boy.

Webster Tuesday Sept. 7 1847

Afternoon I pulled some peas & got in the potatoes that George and girls dug yesterday & to day

—8 We dug some more potatoes

—9th I went to mill in fore noon & went to Little River Ville in afternoon

—10th Dull & rainy

11th dug potatoes in fore noon, some wet in afternoon

Sun 12th Dull,

13th State Election, thick weather yet began to dig potatoes in the fore noon & came on to rain & fell quite smartly in the afternoon, Elisabeth commenced attending a high school at four corners kept by A.J West, Mr. Asa Johnson died to day aged some over eighty years.

—14th dug potatoes

—15th Dug potatoes in fore noon and went to the funeral of Mr. Johson in afternoon, I cut up some corn in fore noon

—16th We dug the potatoes in the pasture piece below the orchard, some frost last night very light

—17th & 18th Threshed some peas & dug potatoes

Sun 19th I did not go to meeting, E. Hinkley & A. Goodwin here, & John Robinson from St Albans here, Mary Ann is getting up sloly, has a cold & bad cough[1], Lucy Farrow here since the 11th inst. and boy

—20th We got in some corn & bean stalks &c. some rain in afternoon

—21st Some rainy I made Elisabeth a pair of thin shoes & husked corn in evening

—22d Dug potatoes in fore noon & went to the funeral of E. Colbys daughter in afternoon

---

1. Mary Ann evidently was confined to bed for more than two weeks following her delivery.

I went to mill & got horses shod in fore noon & dug potatoes in afternoon

—24th I threshed & winnowed nine bushels beans and George & children dug potatoes, cool Southerly wind

—25th got in corn in fore noon, & picked seed corn in afternoon & pulled weeds

—Sun, 26th Dull with some rain R. Dyer here last night

—27th Rainy, husking today,

28th Dull again, husking some & sorted corn, heard that Mr. J. Deering died last night

—29th I & Ann went to Littlriver shoping in fore noon, & dug potatoes in afternoon, I went to mill & we had a severe thunder shower, Hannah Gould came here

30th We dug more potatoes, the ground quite wet, I carried H. Gould home in evening

—Oct 1st We picked seed corn in afternoon.

2d got in corn in afternoon

Sun 3d Not at meeting N. Hinkley here quite pleasant

—4th 5th & 6th husking

7th We got in the last of our corn

—8th & 9th husking

Sun 10th I went to the funeral of Mr. Foxs wife of Sylvanus Falls

—11th I sorted & carried in corn all day

—12th we dug potatoes had a severe rain at night & morning of 13th finished sorting corn to day—No frost to kill all vegetables till the night of the 11th

—14th I & George helpd C. Jordan 2d I was at work boarding his barn & George helping him plow

—15th We hauld some manure in fore noon & finishd diging for potatoes in afternoon

Webster October 16th 1847

I and wife went down to see William & Ebenezer Jordan both being quite sick. William for some time past, E not till quite lately, hauld some manure in for noon & sorted potatoes &C. in afternoon, Amos Davis here,

Sun 17th I went down & shaved William Jordan in the morning & Ann and Elisabeth came down & we went to the funeral of Stephen Andrews son of Ephraim Andrews of Lisbon who died at Lowell, serm. By Eld Bates of Turner

18, 19 and 20th Hauling manure,

21st & 22d in fore noon helpd the Robinsons plow, afternoon of 22 picked over some potatoes, which are roting considerably in the cellar

23d I hauld some manure in fore noon & spread in afternoon.

—Sun 24th I went down to see Ebenezer & William Jordan, & over to N. Js & home in fore noon

25th some rain last night, & foggy this morning William Robinson helpd me break up[1], smart squalls of rain in afternoon & clears off

—26th Reuben Dyer helpd me break up, very cold & windy

—27th Reuben helpd me again, but very cold & freezing last night but more pleasant today

—28th I helpd Mr. Robinson plow peas

—29th I went to Topsham & Brunswick to engage[2] a hog [continued on next page]

---

1 "Break up" means to prepare ground with a spade or plow (OED), probably here the latter.

2 Here, again, "to engage" means that TJ guarantees to deliver a hog in the future at a certain price. The hog was, in fact, slaughtered on November 10th to fulfill the "engagement."

Webster Friday Oct. 29th 1847

I had 8 1/2 cents offered in Topsham & 9 in Brunswick. Quite a pleasant day, I hear to day that old Mrs Ham died on the 21st and buried on the 24th

—39th I helpd Mr Robinson plow again, fine & pleasant
Sun. 31st. I went to four Corners to meeting, serm. by A. J. West, pleasant—

—I have been very busy lately, I shell corn by night & go to mill before day [break]

Nov. 1st Very pleasant indeed I dug carrots, assisted E. Jordan 2d to rig a body on two pair of wheels to haul goods for S. Cushman I cut into house and chimney to put in some lead[1] &c, &c

—2d I hauld some dirt from pig yard, & finishd leading chimney, cleared the back house &c. very warm

—3d Plowed in the pasture west of the old house so calld Very remarkable warm too warm for a plow team
—4th I helped E. Jordan 2d on his barn, finished boarding & began to shingle, some; little rain his morning but unusually pleasant after.
—5th Rainy, cleaned our hog pen, carried cobs out of corn barn, threshed some beans and carried Elisabeh to school in the morning, went to mill & got horse shoe & went after Elisabeth at night
—6th I cleared stuff out of he garden in the morning, some rain afternoon C. Jordan 2d helped me finish plowing the piece in the pasture & haul over some stumps, cloudy cold & windy

---

1 Lead flashing to correct or prevent a leak in the roof.

Webster Sunday Nov. 7th 1847

At home all day, cloudy at night, we are very much broke of our rest by night on account of our boy which we call Albert, being very trouble-some & uneasy night & day

—8th I got S. Coursen to wheel wood into the wood house I got help to haul over the stumps in the pasture in afternoon, had E. Jordan 2d two pair of oxen, William Robinson & one pair, N. Mordan & one pair, and Joseph Blethens oxen, had good luck & got them all over, dull all day, & some rain at night

—9th I got chains mended in fore noon & hauld some manure into the garden in afternoon

—10th Hauld manure & some dirt into the orchard in he forenoon, & N.S. Jordan helpd me to kill & dress our hog that I engaged at Brunswick some time since

—11th I went to B[runswick]. with the hog and a firkin of Butter E. Swett had the hog who weighted 545lb and N. Perkins had the butter 80 1/2 lb. Received 9 cents for the pork & 18 for butter

—12th I helpd Mr Marr kill a hog in fore noon,, I shelld corn & went to mill in afternoon, & prepared and tied up all the cattle for the first time

—13th I went down & help'd Wm. Buckman raise a barn frame on his 2d farm in fore noon, & hauled some manure from the hog pen in afternoon, heard that young H. Corbet died to day

Webster Sunday Nov 14th 1847

Snowing this morning early& continued to storm the most of the day, quite a snow at night, I was effected with a diziness in the head

—15th Some stormy in the fore noon & carried Elisabeth over to school in the morning & bought 14 1/2 lb sole leather of P. M. Garcelon, I picked out pea straw &c. saw'd some wood & the like went over after Elisabeth at night, not so good sleighing as in the morning

—16th We killd our hog & pig S. Coursen help'd, cool in the morning but rather a pleasant sun through the day, I am still troubled with the diziness in my head, and feel some degree of interest as the cause of it, having never before had a like feeling when I have had some diziness in my head

—17th I cut up & salted pork, rather a pleasant day

—18thRather dull, hauld off some stone up by the ledge & hauld manure from the hog pen

—9th Some rain & cut & closed a pair of shoes for Rowena, went over after Elisabeth she had boarded to Mr. West's for a few days, and the school closed today, very mudy indeed, the snow has about all disappeared

20th I bottomed Rowena's shoes, clear & cooler

—Suund 21st at home all day, some diziness in the head yet. I have showered my head & taken some pills for physic

Webster Monday Nov. 22d 1847

I went up t Capt. Woodburys to se a yearlin steer & went up to see Dr Cutter, he tells me that I must live sparingly & keep the bowels loose & tha it would be well to take some blood[1], very remarkable pleasant in the afternoon I banked up a part of the house

—23d Dull & misty, I banked up the remainder of the house in fore noon & whet Mrs. Lord's wood saw in afternoon & N Jordans

—24th dull, foggy & some misty, E. Jordan 2d help'd haul dirt from the hill down in the passage at the end of the cornbarn, & from the pigyard in to the field, very smart rain at night

—25th Anual Thanksgiving, some sun but more cloud, I jobd round set gate post, hauld potatoe tops &c. Marriage ceremony performed at Mr. Starrs today

—26th Clears off this morning as pleasant as a June morning, so warm & pleasant that meat has flyblown[2] to day in the cheese room, S Coursen help me haul dirt into the field between the round top & long sweet apple trees

—26th Cull and raw all day I did not go to meeting,

29th Very cold & windy I picked over potatoes in fore noon & went over to the town house, having been notified that it was finishd & found it all completed & as per contract

---

1 Although physicians were beginning to question the value of therapeutic blood-letting, it was in use until the Civil War. Except for a few conditions (e.g. chronic congestive heart failure, polycytemia vera, etc.) phlebotomy did no good and could be harmful.

2 "flyblow" refers to the deposition of eggs by flies and "flyblown" refers to the presencee of eggs, or more likely, maggots. Animals were slaughtered in the late fall depending on seasonal cold for refrigeration. With unseasonably warm weather, however, flies become active.

Webster Nov 30th 1848

Very cold & freezing last night, the first night that any thing has froze in the barn this fall—I got the vinegar into the cellar & picked over potatoes

—Dec 1st made ready in fore noon to go to Bath, but the weather did not look right, with a smart southerly breeze, & so concluded not to go, I tapd shoes for Ann & Elisabeth in afternoon, very thick & cloudy in evening

—2d Rainy all day I tapd shoes again, foggy & rainy at night
3d I picked over potatoes the most of the day, rather pleaasant
—4th I picked over potatoes again
—Sun. Dull, Rush with Jordan of Danville came over to commence our school toorrow, I went up to B. Dyers in afternoon
—6th Snowing this morning early & it fell smartly all the forenoon, rather damp too, I went down to Colbys shop in forenoon & over to J Haskals & got six bushels coals for Colby to iron my pung.[1]

—7th Clear & pleasant I went to mill in afternoon & got some wood into the wood house

—8th I helpd Colby on my pung
—9th I went over to Henry Carvills early in the morning & paid him twenty five dollars for the town house lot and got the deed, I went over to Mr Hendersons to see him concerning the acceptance of the town house & over to P.M. Garcelons & talked with him about it, he refused to grant an order because of an exception as to time

---

1 "….iron my pung." would mean adding iron sheatiing to the sled's runners.

Webster December 10th 1847

I helpd Colby again, foggy & misty

—11th I helpd Colby some rain, very werm indeed & very mudy, no frost in the ground, caterpillars crawling lively—I got home from Colbys at eleven of the clock P.M. & then it was clear & not freezing any

—12th I went over to meeting in fore noon, uncommon pleasant for the season, did not need any mittens going, nor coming home, the sun pleasant & warm as September on the 7th it was qu[i]te fine sleighing & to day there is no snow to be seen, nor any frost & mud enough

—13th I went up to Capt. Woodburys & changed a one year old steer with him & paid three dollars between them. Dull today & dreadful mudy, afternoon I went down to Colby's & bought home my pung bottom

—14th At work on a pung top more rain

—15th Clears off to day & rather cooler, I went over to N.J.s in evening Hannah is more feeble, freezing some in evening

—16th Quite fine, at work on pung top

—17th Storming early, of sleet & falling most of the day

—18th Some snow today in fore noon, more pleasnt in afternoon, I finishd the pung top and painted it in the evening

—Sun. 19. Rather moderate no one of us at meeting to day

—20th I got horse shod at Colbys & got the last of the work done on pung bottom, cold & some snow, I put irons on pung fills[1] & painted them.

---

1 The "fills" were the shafts between which the horse stood.

Webster Dec. Tuesday 21st 1847

Reuben Dyer & C Coursen helpd me chop wood in the woods quite cool

—22d Cold & some snow in forenoon, Reuben D & S. Coursen & I went up to J. Blethens in the morning after a sow pig that I carried up last night, Reuben & I chopd today

—23d I went over to four corners & bought an ax of S. Cushman, ground it and chop'd with Reuben & S. Coursen. I heard that Enoch Hinkley's Benjamin was drowned yesterday in Bath

—24th Reuben & Coursen helpd me chop again, moderate

—25 I & Coursen chopd again, I did not go over to meeting in the evening. Reuben Elisabeth & Rowena went over; cool with N.E. wind

Sun 26th I did not go to meeting, some little snow last night & cool today

27th Clear & cold I went down to Colbys & got hooks staples &c made for pung top, put them on & painted the pung in afternoon

—28th Quite a snow in forenoon light & dry, I went into the woods with team for the first time, in afternoon the swamp bore the team quite well

—29th I hauld six load of wood. S. Coursen helpd me, very pleasant & the snow is getting soft, F.D. Wentworth & wife & Mr. Walton & wife here on an evening visit.

—39th very pleasant I hauld poles & logs, the snow is soft & all gone in the road at night.

—31st No frost last night. I got ready & went to Topsham to market

I got down to Topsham about noon, so warm as not need an over coat, sold potatoes for 68 cent, oats for 50 cts butter for 18 cts, cabbage for 6cts & sage for 25 cts got home the first part of the evening, more muddy in evening than morning, the horse would break through the frost often, & also the waggon in many places

January 1st 1848

No frost again last night, dull & foggy this morning, the snow is mostly gone, & mud is plenty. I tap'd Reuben Dyers boots in fore noon & went to mill in afternoon & got a chain mended at Colbys, some misty just as night, picked over potatoes in evening.

Sun 2d Quite rainy the most of the day & smartly sometimes, scarcely an atom of snow to be seen & the frost leaving the ground rapidly, I have no recollection of so warm a turn at this season,

—3d I chopd wood in the woods, pleasant & no frost in the wood

—4th At work fixing an ox yoke for E. Jordan 2d & hewd out a piece for a steers yoke

—5th I chopd wood again in the woods & clearing a road into the most N.W. part of woodland, came on o snow just as night, fine & light

—6th I hauld out some poles in forenoon, very cool & finishd the steers yoke in afternoon, 2 or 3 in[ches] snow

—7th I hauld wood

—8th I hauld wood again snowing all day—snowed smartly in the evening

Webster Sunday January 9th 1848

Rains smartly this morning, clears off pleasant & moderate. R Dyer came down & I & Ann went home with him, the snow is very soft and the sleigh cuts through very much, grows cooler at night

—10th I got up early & put up some potatoes & went to Bath, very cold and windy. The sleighing good to Topsham & none from there to Bath. I got into Bath late, sold out & started for home just before sunset extremely cold comeing home.

—11th & 12th I was at work for J. Blethen making wood sled, the 11th was very cold & 12th pleasant

—13th I hauld wood.

—14th I hauld two load of wood in fore noon. Mr. J Gould & wife up here, moderate & misty in fore noon & some rain in afternoon

—15th Some rain in fore noon I went to mill & went down to Tuttles in Durham & got an ax new laid[1] quite rainy in afternoon & evening did not get home till in evening, sleighing very poor indeed when I came home

—Sun. 16th Clear & very pleasant the ground thaws, and the sun is spring like

—17th I boiled the ends of a new yoke and oiled them to prevent checking[2], Silas Jordan came up at noon & helpd me grind the new ax, and I got out some stuff for ox bows & turned them in the evening one pair of horn beam[3] that turned well, the first I ever saw

—19th I chopd in the woods in fore noon & worked of steers bows & put staple[4] in steers yoke &c in afternoon

—19th Nathaniel Gillpatrick helpd me chop in [continued on following page]

---

1 The term "lay" is old and means having the edge of a cutting instrument "re-steeled." Steel was welded along the edge of tools, a technique seldom used today, but common in the past. Steel would hold an edge, unlike the soft iron used for the axe head.

2 "Check" in this sense means "to split or crack." OED.

3 Hornbeams (there are two separate species) are trees in the birch family noted for their close-grained, hard wood. Apparently TJ was using hornbeam for the bows and he was able to bend the wood into the shape he wanted.

4 TJ's "staple" would have been s U-shaped or ring-like contrivance attached to the center of the underside of the cross-piece (beam) of the yoke to which a chain or rope was attached for leading the oxen.

Webster Thursday Jan. 20th 1848

in woods for Joseph Blethen, quite cool

—20th I shod one side of the bobsled, quite pleasant

—21st & 22d I was at work getting out stuff for a horse rake[1]

—Sun. 23d Pleasant and the ground froze hard & all bare. I went over to meeting on horse back

—24th At work a little on the horse rake we went up to Amos Davis' in the evening, in a waggon the ground on road was not very rough but very hard. Carried Holman & left Albert with the children, heard of the death of Mr Hill & old Mr Coburn of Greene & of Mr Woodside of Wales, Col David Chenneys wife was buried on Sunday.

—25th At work on the horse rake, but little prospect of snow, Susan Jordan is quite sick we were down to see her last Sunday evening & she appeared quite feeble.

26th & 27th At work on & finished horse rake-dull & some sleet & snow

—28th pleasant, began to make a yoke for E. Jordan2d & Mr Pettengill came, fine fair sleighing this morning, soon after a man calling his name Nathl. Warren came & claimed the horse I had of Albert Warren on the 13th of July last saying he bought the horse & let his brother Albert have him & to be his brothers when he paid for him but was his until then, he left & I & Mr. Pettengill went up to the mills to se J. Hill Esq he being from home we came back & soon this Warren calld again [continued on following page]

---

1 "horse-rake "an agricultural implement [rake] mounted on wheels and drawn by a horse...." OED.

& then said he should sue me before he left I told him he could do as he pleased about that, but I would go up to Esq. Hills and if he would meet me there we would talk more about it. I went up & he met me there & then confesed that the bill of sale as he calld it that he took of the man he had the horse of had been obtained recently for to use on this occasion, & that he and his brother gave their joint note for the horse on the 24 of December 1846 and that he had it to pay, and finally consented to give me the month of February to investigate the matter & left at that

29th I began upon the yoke again & set it all out & attempted to take an [a]uger & behold that was gone, I then yoked the oxen & went into the woods & hauled out three logs for school house wood & then C Haskal came to amend the Constitution of the Universalist Society of Lisbon, he and I having been chosen for that purpose at the annual meeting of the Society. We wrote off a constitution & went over to the adjourned meeting & adjourned again to meet at the meeting house in two weeks no sleighing today.

Sun. 30th We went up to B. Dyers & carried Holman & Albert in the waggon very pleasant, when we got home heard that Hannah Jordan was very sick & so we went over to se [sic] her in the evening & found her very bad indeed, also heard [continued on next page]

that Susan J. was failing

—Jan31st I went over to see Hannah & found her alive & some brighter. & calld to see Susan who was very feeble indeed. I made E Jordan 2d an ox yoke in afternoon, We went over to see Hannah in evening no alteration

—Feb 1st Began to snow in the morning. I shelled corn &c. Mary Ann went down & watched with Hannah & I took care of the baby, we heard by the children from school that Susan was growing worse.
2d When Mary Ann came home she brings the news that Susan is dead & Hannah about the same. I went directly down to Eben's but they did not want any assistance for the day but I promsed to go down & set up at night—the snow is blown all about & no sleighing—I went to mill & carried two bushels corn for the pigs, commencing to fat them. While going down to E. Jordan's I discoverd a light in the east which I supposed to be a building on fire, I and Job Atwood watched for the night, thick & moderate, I came home early.
3d we heard that Hannah died last night about midnight, & I went directly over to render assistance if needed, came home & went to Little riverville to get a coat cut very poor sleighing indeed & thawy. I calld to see James Ham who was confined with a broken leg
—4th Made preparations in fore noon & went to the funeral of Susan Jordan at 12 oclock at noon.

Webster Friday Feb. 4th 1848

Serm. By Eld. Day at the funeral of Susan Jordan. I heard to day that the light I saw on 2d was the barn of Nathaniel Gillpatrick being burnt with ten tons of hay one pair of oxen & two cows, sheep, geese &c., Mr Pettengill & wife & A. Davis & wife stayed with us, snowing in evening

5th A smart snow storm this morning & continues through the day, we went down to N. Jordans to the funeral of Hannah. Eld Hanscom preached from first Philippians & 21st verse.

—6th Sunday. Quite a snow storm & blow all day, we broke out the roads nowtwithstanding, self & two pair of oxen two & half hours[1], the snow is considerably drifted into he road

—7th & 8th I hauld wood, nearly a foot of snow in the woods—quite cool

—9th I went over to Raymond & back & got two sett of cart spokes, rather poor sleighing after leaving New Gloucester, got home about eleven in the evening. Ira Farrow had been here & infomed our folks that his wife was dead & he had brought the corpse with him for burial

—10th We went down to John Goulds to the funeral of Mrs Farrow, pleasant in the morning but quite cool in afternoon

—11th I shoveled out the road & repaired bare spots two & half hours—P.M. I helpd Wm. Robinson haul out logs, cold & windy as well as last night

---

1 When TJ works on the road he usually mentions details—one or two pair of oxen and the number of hours that he worked—suggesting that he was paid for the work, or as he mentions earlier that what he earned was subtracted from his town tax.

Enoch Hinkley wife & three children came here yesterday & he helpd me haul wood to day, rather pleasant, Sun 13th We heard early this morning that Wm Jordans wife died very suddenly, Ann carried Enoch & wife over to A. Goodwins in afternoon & we went up to Wm Jordans after she came back with the horse

—14th I hauld wood in forfe noon & we went to the funeral of Mrs. Jordan in afternoon, large meeting, I went to Lombard's mill in evening to mill & to see J. Hill Esq. on account of the claim of W. on my horse —15th I went down to the S. W. B.[1] with Potatoes, could not get but 40 cents offer'd carried them to Little River & sold them for 50 made arrangements to start for Norridgewock[2] tomorrow

16th I went over to Mr. Woodburys & took dinner & down to Gardiner & bought a pair of cart hubs & up to Augusta & stopd the night at Josselyns fine pleasant day, I saw Mr Pullen in evening & found the grave stones he had made for me. I took supper at his house

—17th I went up to Norridgewock. Warren was or had gone to Bangor I saw the Mr. Seldens & found that they understood that N. Warren bought the horse of them, although Albert signed the Notes. I left the business with Mr. Selden [continued on following page]

---

1 S.W.B. = South West Bend on the Androscoggin River.
2 Norridgewock—approximately fifty miles due north of Webster, a long day's trip.

and started for home & came as far as Belgrade hill & stayed all night at the tavern where was a young man that had his foot crushed all to pieces yesterday & had a part of it amputated to day

—18th I came as far as Augusta in fore noon & loaded six set of gravestones took dinner at Mr. Pullens & come to Mr. Woodburys I fell in with & chartered Isaac Jenkins to haul three set of grave stones to his house from within a mile of Hallowell

—19th I came home & found all well & Cousin John & Abigail Jordan from Cape Elizabeth, very pleasant indeed, very poor sleighing from from Potters in Wales, but very good indeed to Norridgewock from there —Sun. 20th dull in fore noon & began to snow in afternoon. The week past has been an unusual pleasant one for season, as it is not uncommon to be the severest part of the winter

—21st I got out a set of cast iron spokes

—22d John & Abigail & Ann went up to J. Pettengills & went after Dr. Cutter to see our Albert who has been quite unwell of late, I shelld corn &c.

23d I shelld corn, repaired corn sheller & champered[1] cart hubs for setting spokes

—24th I went to Little river with potatoes in a waggon & got a barrel of mackerel for which I paid $7.25

—25th I hauld four load of wood quite cool & poor sleding

---

1 "champered"; we would say "chamfered" today. To chamfer may mean either to cut a channel or furrow, or to round off a square edge. OED.

I haul two load of wood in fore noon & the last or all there was chopd.
Ann went over t the four Corners & got a letter from Mr Selden of
Norridgewock the gentleman I conferred with when there to see Mr.
Warren. He writes that Mr. Warren exa[c]ts[1] the whole pay for the
horse I went up to the mills in afternoon, very pleasant & no sleighing

—27th Fair & pleasant, at home all day,

28th I went over to four corners & put two letters in the office one for
E.C. Seldon & one for N. Warren, & then went down to Factory Ville
to N. Hinkley about some money & up to N. Foss and received
ballance due on his note, very pleasant sun & cool air, in fore noon, but
clouds up very quick in afternoon & snows before sunset. I chopd
green wood in afternoon & got it in woodhouse
—29th Some snow in he morning & snow'd all day & very fast at times
I got out cart spokes ready to set
—March 1st Clear & high wind, the snow drifts considerable, I drove
cart spokes Cape John J. helpd'd me[2]

—2d I broke roads two hours with two pairs of oxen and then floord[3]
off wheels & finish'd spokes
—3d At work on wheels, quite windy & some snow

—4th At work on wheels & whet N. J's hand saw very windy in for
noon, the snow drifted. Wm. R. [?] broke out [continued on following
page?]

---

1 "exacts" in this context means "demands." OED. The business about Warren's horse is
confusing. On July 10th TJ wrote that he "changed horses with Warren." As nearly as I
can make out, Albert Warren traded the horse with TJ. It then turned out that the horse
belonged to his brother Nathaniel Warren, and Nathaniel wants to be paid for the horse.

2. As TJ noted above, his cousin John Jordan is visiting from Cape Elizabeth

3 "to place *upon* (something) as a floor." OED; i.e., TJ placed the wheels on the floor so he
could work on the spokes.

Webster Sun. March 5th 1848

Snowing early but clears off & I & Ann went over to meeting. The wind springs up & blows smart with snow squalls, came home, no meeting smart wind all day & the snow blows merrily, more winterlike weather than any yet & more snow than at any one time before The road full & no traveling, I intended to have gone to Wales after the grave stones left there on the 3d, but poor sleighing. I saw in the paper to day the death of John Q. Adams[1] on the 23d ult. at Washington

—6th Broke out roads in fore noon self & two pair oxen afternoon carried Abigail over to N.Js. and then went to mill & over to four corners got town orders for town house services & for money advance to pay for town house lot to H. Carvill, changed my mind about going to Portland intend to go to Bath tomorrow

—7th I went to Bath & carried eight bushels beans & two hams of bacon, got 8 ½ cents for bacon and $1.42 for beans, got iron for cart wheels, stayed at E. Hinkly's at night, very pleasant
8th Came home, very warm
—9th Rainy & very soft at work on wheels
—10 Snowing & drifting J. Blethen returned from Portland left his horse with me, could not get home, at work on wheels to day drove spokes in J. Davis' hubs

---

1 John Quincy Adams (1767-1848), President of the United States (1825-1849). Interestingly, it took ten days for news of Adams death to reach Webster, Maine, from Washington, D.C.. Although Samuel Finley Breese Morse (1791-1872) had invented the telegraph in 1837 it required further technical development before coming into general use during the Civil War in the 1860s.

Webster Saturday March 11th 1848

I broke out roads two hours myself & oxen two pair in for noon & went up to Wales after grave stones Ann went up to W. Jordans with me, pleasant & tolerable sleighing

—Sun. 12th We went down to Mr Jacob Goulds very pleasant in fore noon, clouds up suddenly & snows at dark

—13th Dull at three oclock & I started for Freeport the little snow made fine sleighing, I got .65 cents for potatoes in cash & four bushels of plaster for one of potatoes got home at half past one in afternoon

—14th I went to Norridgewock & settled with Warren for my horse that evening, very cold riding stayed at Sawyers tavern

—15 I started for home soon after seven oclock in the morning & got home early in the evening, very cold to day

—16th at work on J. Davis' wheels

17th I went to Little River & carried a barrel to get a barrel of molasses.[1] Mr. Davis too full of business to attend to it, snowing smartly & every appearance of a severe storm, afternoon at work on wheels

—18th I got the rimming on one of J. Davis wheels

—Sun. 19th I went to meeting very fine and pleasant

—20th I went to Freeport carried ten bushels seed potatoes & got 65 cents cash Jesse & Benjamin Davis went with me the little snow last night made the sleighing tolerable, warm sun & mud & water a plenty comeing home

---

1 Molasses was an important staple in New England cooking, used well into the twentieth century for baking—ginger cookies, brown bread, ginger-bread, etc.—and for Indian puddings, mince meat, poured over rice and over bread as a desert, and in many other ways where sugar would be used today.

Webster Tuesday March 21st 1848

I whet wood saw for Wm. Jordan in fore noon & killd & dressed a pig in afternoon

—22d I went to Brunswick with pig. Sold to Lemont & Hall for 8 3/0 [?] cents weighing 327 llb very poor wheeling indeed I brought a barrel of molasses from Little River home

—23d A. Davis & wife here on a visit, did nothing to day but to read Coolidge's trial[1]

—24th We went to Little River shoping took dinner at J. Hams we calld to see Aunt Sally Jordan on our return who is very low & feeble

—25th I went down again early & she appeared to be failing. We went to Mr. Pettengills, & carried Holman & Albert, stoped & took dinner & came home early their little girl having the hooping cough, Ann went down to E. Jordan; his mother die in a few minutes after she arrived. I was rather unwell at night

—Sun 26th I went down to E. Jordan's in forenoon, came up to Mr Weymouths to get him to take the management of the funeral tomorrow at ten oclock & agreed to get the hearse & someone or more to watch to night, I and William Robinson watched there at night

—27th Came home early & after breakfast I went after the hearse for E. Jordan and went down to funeral at ten oclock, serm by A.J. West, came on to rain about the time the procession was formed.

---

1 It would take an unusual event to occupy TJ's interest to this extent, and Coolidge's trial certainly qualified. Valorous P. Coolidge was a physician of Waterville, Maine who had applied to one Edward Mathews for a loan. Mathews refused to advance funds to the overextended doctor. Coolidge then offered Mathews a libation. Mathews accepted and rapidly succumbed, for the brandy had been laced with prussic (HCN, hydrocyanic) acid. Ironically, Coolidge was called on to determine the cause of Mathew's sudden death. The doctor conducted a post-mortem examination and even though he hid the victim's eroded stomach he was discovered, tried and found guilty—whereupon he took his own life. Needless to say, the trial, the events leading up to it, and its outcome excited great interest, all the more so because the murderer and his victim apparently were black. Lurid accounts of the affair were published both in contemporary newspapers and later in a pamphlet, *Trial of Dr. Valorous P. Coolidge for the Murder of Edward Mathews, at Waterville, Maine*, 1850.

Webster Monday March 27

Afternoon went down to Colbys & got horse shod, rainy

—28th Rainy all day at work on Jon L Davis' wheels

29th Clears off in fore noon, doweled wheels, pleasant

—Sun 30th Finishd one wheel in fore noon & killd a pig in afternoon

—31st I started early & went to Brunswick with the pig, sold to Sewell for 8 ¾ cents per lb weighed 371 lb, I brought Elisabeth Carvill up from Bunswick, very muddy indeed

April 1st, I finsh'd the other wheel of J.P. Davis in fore noon & went to mill in afternoon & went to school meeting. chose a committee to select some place to remove the school house to & adjourned to meet again on the fifth

—Sun. 2d I went to meeting but one discourse, Mr West - last discourse with us

—3d I painted a part of the portch floor & doweled my wheels, very pleasant & drying

—4th & 5th at work on wheels &c. went to school meeting on 5th

6th Niah Hinkley & I chopd wood at the door very windy

—7th Niah is sick & I chopd wood at the door again still windy

—8th More pleasant, Niah & I chop'd wood & finished it

—Sun. 9th Ann carried Niah home, pleasant—I was up to see Joseph Blethen who has been quite sick but is better & over N. Jordans

—10th Silas Jordan helpd me split wood

Webster Tuesday April 11th 1848

I began a pair of wheels for Daniel Cary & Silas J. split wood again

—12th Silas J. helpd me, he chopd school house wood & helpd me set the spokes in Carys hubs

—13th 14h & 15th At work on s[ai]d. Wheels & got them nearly done

—Sun. 16th We went down to Niah Hinkleys

17th I went to Freeport with potatoes and got .65 cents per bushel

—18th I went to Freeport again with potatoes very cold last night

—19th Some snow last night, I finished C.s wheels & helpd N. Jordan frame

—20th I went down to Littleriver with eight bushels potatoes to Bibber & helpd N. Jordan again

—21st I tap'd my boots & painted wheels &c.

—22d I went up to Mr Stanfords to carry up leather for a pair of thin boots & to mill & over to four corners & bought a plow & up to E. Jordans 2d after my yoke in fore noon & afternoon I harrowed & sowd the potatoe ground in the pasture below the orchard & was taken quite unwell relax[1] & vomiting

—Sun. 23d Quite unwell,

24th Still unwell but harrowd some above the barn, Benjamin Randall agreed

to work for me half of the time commencing May first.

25th Very unwell last night, harrowd more in afternoon

—26th I harrowd for oats by what we call the old house, quite dry

---

1 TJ evidently uses "relax" to mean "weak."

Webster April 27th Thursday

I sowd oats & harrowd & rolld the ground quite pleasant. Mr Clough buried to day

—28th I dug corn buts

—29th I beat the dirt off some buts & came on rainy

Sun 30th At home

May1st B. Randall began work we plowd the garden & some by the yard & furrowed some & put out some manure for potatoes above the barn

—2d Quite rainy in fore noon & hauld off some stone in afternoon & sold our oxen to C.P. Mitchell for $85 we put out some manure

—3d We set five set of gravestones in fore noon & planted some potatoes in afternoon

rth Very rainy indeed all day, saw'd some school wood &c.

5th Planted some potatoes & put some manure, Wm Robinson carried steer up to J. Cushings to help move his barn

—6th Hauld manure in fore noon & plow'd for corn in afternoon some showery the ground quite wet.

Sun. 7th Not very well took physick

8th Washington Jordan helpd me get the buts off of the wheat ground & cultivate it in the afternoon

9th I made garden & help'd N. J raise his portch

10th Sowd one & half bushel wheat & one bushel of oats harrowd & rolld the ground

—11th Very rainy indeed which makes the ground very wet indeed

Webster Friday May 12th 1848

I got horse shod & went to mill, hauld logs to mill &c

13th I went over to B. Dyers & got his steers & harrow'd on the corn ground by sweet appletrees, the ground wet & heavy

—Sun 14th We went to meeting serm by Eld D.T. Stevens The first sabbath on engagement for the season, some rain his morning, but cloudy & cool after

—15th B. Randall came again & we cut fencing & hauld to fence the potatoe ground in the pasture, cool & windy, weighed hay for R. Dyer & sold H. Garcelon a set of cart spokes

—16th Some rain in the morning but we hauld manure & plowed for corn on a piece between the two upper gates, rather heavy to plow

—17th Finished the corn ground & harrowd on broke up ground by old sweet appletree in fore noon, & got of buts [beets?] & cultivated & harrow'd the ground by the spring below the sweet appletree

—18th I sow'd half bushel wheat on the above piece & the remainder to oats harrowd & rolled it in fore noon, we furrowd some in fore noon & Randall put in some manure, & afternoon we put in manure & cover'd some corn, very warm and pleasant

—19th Very warm & growing, we put manure, covered corn & harrowd the corn ground after rolling between the two upper gates

—20th Mr. Spears help'd us for E. Jordan, nearly finish'd planting, some fine rain by spells, work'd about all the time

Webster Sunday May 21st 1848

At home all day, Some rain again to day, very fine for grass, vegetation has come forward very rapidly since the warm weather for the last week

—22d Some rain & hauld a maple log to mill & got hemlock boards, hauld down some manure & put in the garden

—23d I went up to Mr Wentworths to change some potatgoes, holed for potatgoes between corn & potatoes by first gate in fore noon & put in manure in afternoon, & hauld some old manure down in the field

—24th hauld down some new manure to spread & hauld off stone on the new piece in the pasture & harrowd Wm Robinson help'd me to plow the piece I hauld the manure on

—26 I cross harrow'd the pasture piece in fore noon & We went to Little River Ville in afternoon

27th Planted Mangelwortzel in fore noon put sticks on corn ground &c. Afternoon hauld some stuff & fenc'd on the pasture piece; Rather raw & cool the most of the week

—Sunday 28th We went to meeting in fore noon & to the funeral of Mr. Roberts child in afternoon. Eld Stephens preachd dull in the morning but rather a pleasant day

—29th planted the pasture piece to potatoes & harrowd the little piece in the field

—30th Very great rain indeed, amazing wet

Webster Wednesday May 31st 1848

We set the iron posts for a length of picket fence at the western side of the field in fore noon & poled some fence by old sweet apple tree, afternoon we put top poles on the pasture fence by Mr. Davis woods, windy & very cold

—June 1st I went to the mill & got some joist, stop'd[1] some fence in fore noon & planted potatoes on the piece that Mr Robinson help'd me plow on 25 ult. Very uncommon cold this afternoon for the season, finished planting potatoes

—2d I striped[2] the roof of the shed or a part of it prepared zinc[3] to put on the roof at the barn, went over to N. J's I got some nails, laid a few shingles &c. quite pleasant to day, but very hard frost last night in some places

—3d I laid shingles on shed roof, very fine & pleasant

—Sun. 4 Very fine, Niah H. & wife, two children & Sarah Goodwin up here, grass looks foreward, & apple trees were in full bloom last week throug[h] the cold & frost

—5th Very fine & I shingled on the shed

—6th very rainy I put zinc on roof of shed & over barn doors, split oven wood &c.

—7th More rain by showers, I shelld corn, wheel'd manure into the yard &c.

*th Dull with dashes of rain I went to the factory & got horse shod at D. Jones in fore noon & planted beans with the corn in afternoon. The corn being up.

9th I planted beans in for noon. I went up to B. Dyers early after Reuben to help on road

---

1 TJ repaired the fence by "stopping," *i.e.* closing, the holes in it.

2 The "striping" consisted of marking or chalking the roof to indicate where each course of shingles would go.

3 The zinc would have been in malleable sheets, used on peak of roof and elsewhere as flashing to prevent water leaks. Zinc would not rust. Copper sheathing is usually used for the same purpose today.

Webster Friday June 9th 1848

Afternoon at work on the road, some spatters of rain from N.E.

10th At work on the road, plowing & hauling off the McKenney hill, last night I was down on the ridge to see Niah & to get him to help me next week on the road.

Sun 11th Very fine save a high wind in afternoon for a spell, at home when I ought to have been to meeting, no excuse but being fatigued & dull among people not done planting yet round about

—12th Pealed some hemlock bark very cold with big wind & very drying

—13th & 24 th At work on the road more pleasant

—15th Harrowed potatoes & the corn by sweet apple trees in fore noon & I layed shingles on the shed in afternoon & Randall R. Dyer hoed potatoes

16th I finished the shed, quite fine

—17th I sheared sheep. B. Randall who went home on the 15 came back this morning and desired to quit work & so I settled up

Sun 18th We went up to Mr Dyers

—19th I hoed potatoes above the barn, very warm.

—20th Some rain S. Coursen helpd me a part of the day, finish'd the piece of potatoes above the barn

—21st hoed corn on the upper piece

—22d I finish'd the upper piece of corn

—3d I & Samuel Robinson went down to George Rogers in Topsham at a hearing [continued on next page]

117

of the parties before a committee appointed by Court to reverse or affirm the decision of County Commissioners las[t] fall on the bay bridge road lying in Topsham & Bowdoin, the Commissioners discontinued & the Committee reversed their decission.

24th I wed corn very windy

—Sun 25th At meeting, Serm by Eld Stephens, some little rain & clear afternoon
—26th & 27th I wed corn & finish'd fine hoe time
—28th I went down to Colbys early to get horse shod, could not then came home & went up to Carvills to see about getting my cart tyre set, came home & got horse shod at Colby's, at work fitting ox bows &c in afternoon
—29th I got my new wheels ironed at Carvills by S Nicols, some rain yesterday & more this fore noon—very warm sun in afternoon
—3i0th I fitted old cart ex[1] in the new wheels, at work in the garden &c.

July 1st I hoed some potatoes in fore noon, the Peach blows[2], afternoon I got some work done at Colby s & put clogs[3] in axletree for the new wheels
Sund. 2d At home all day

—3d I hauld a rock maple log to the mill in fore noon some rain & made a bolster[4] to the waggon in the afternoon, more rain

—4th Very fine & pleasant in the morning [continued on next page]

—————————
1 The OED gives "ex" as a colloquialism for "axe," but in this context it would have to be "axle"

2 "blows" means "blossoms"

3 The generic meaning of "clog" is something that impedes action. A block of wood with a curved face was often used to brake wagons or other conveyances. It was attached to a lever arm that would force the block against the wheel. TJ may have been referring to a friction brake of this type, although one would not expect it to be attached directly to the axletree.

4 A "bolster"was a "transverse bar over the axle of a wagon which supports the bed, and raises it from the axle" OED

Webster Tuesday July 4th 1848

We went up to Lewiston falls in company with Samuel Robinson & wife & Amos Davis & wife to see & hear what we could, the first we heard after we arrived was, that a young man by the name of Herrick had his thigh broke & his leg much injured by the bursting of a cannon, so bad was he that it was thought necessary to amputate & was & I saw the leg & thigh in afternoon at Dr. G[arcelon]'s Office[1]; we went over to the Congregational M[eeting]. H[ouse]. to an Oration by Lawyer Chase, then took dinner at Davis inn after waiting some time, then we rode out by E. Littles Esq. to the rail road by the burying ground, & then down the hill & out to embankment by the foundry, & up on the deep cut & embankments out to the river. where the rail road bridge is to be built then back & into the foundry, from thence across the bridge & I went up to the abutment of the rail road bridge on the eastern shore, nearly completed, a great work.[2] Then up the cut & back to the brick block where Mary Ann was in waiting & started for home, having nearly spent the day in seeing & hearing & quite well satisfied at that, for excepting the said accident refered to above. The day passd off finely. The procession of Martha Washingtons & Recabites[3] at the Oration, & the good order & sobriety of the people was very creditable

---

1 We wish that TJ had told us a little more. Sulfuric (diethyl) ether had been introduced into medicine on October 16th, 1846 at the Massachusetts General Hospital in Boston during the first public demonstration of its use as a surgical anesthetic. It was quickly adopted. We have to wonder whether it was used for this surgery.

2 TJ does not mention the name of the railroad company that was constructing this line. A 1908 Geological Survey map of 1908 shows both the Grand Trunk and Maine Central as serving Auburn/Lewiston.

3 The "Martha Washingtons" were a patriotic women's group. His "Recabites" evidently refers to the Rebeccaites, a protest organization active in Wales, England, during the first half of the 19th century. It was made up of men disguised as women, hence the name. I have been unable to find out anything about Rebeccaite activity in America.

Webster Wednesday July 5th 1848

I hoed potatoes over in the pasture & Jordan 2d helpd me a part of the
for noon quite fine

—6th Reuben Dyer helpd me in fore noon, some showers of mist &
afternoon showers of rain so that we did not how any

—7th we finshd the piece on the pasture & hoed the most of a small
piece in the field in the fore noon, & afternoon I went to Little
riverville & bought a barrel of flour for which I paid $6.12 & a hay
fork &c. &c.

—8th I went down to E. Colbys with horse rake to get irons fitted very
fine indeed, afternoon I put irons on horse rake, put one of the racks
together &c.

Sun. 9th I was at meeting serm by Mr Osgood of Auburn quite a fine
day

—10th I went up to the mills in fore noon to mill & after rolls, to[o]
dull to commence haying afternoon put the rack together

—11th I bagan to mow east of the house, some in fore & afternoon,
raked up what I mowed in fore noon with the new horse rake—very
warm

—12th I mowd in the old garden & orchard, very warm again I got in
two loads of hay Elizabeth helping

—13th I mowd again foggy in fore noon spread & raked what I mow

—14th I did not mow any very foggy in fore

—15th I mowd & raked up & left in winrow

Sun. 16th Some appearance of a shower in fore noon, I put up the hay
left in winrow last night, some little rain

Webster Monday July 17th 1848

I mowd again & got in two load, no other help than Elisabeth

18th Wm Coursen help'd me fine hay weather

—19th 20th 21st & 22d Reuben Dyer & S. Coursen helpd me got along finely some appearance of a storm on 22d very strong south wind in afternoon, we put up in the swamp & on the side hill below old sweet appletree

—Sun 23d very [adjective missing] in the morning Eld Stephens came in & soon began to rain he & I went over to the meeting house & no one there we went down to Mr. Garcelons rained some in going & very smartly while there, took dinner & stayed a part of the afternoon we came home, & after tea Mr Stephens went home

—24th I went to mill in fore noon, some rain, afternoon I wed garden, had a shower in afternoon & another in evening with sharp lightning & heavy thunder, with wind to break down the corn

—25th I went up to the mills after rolls, no appearance of hay weather, I mowed in afternoon, Mr. Frost brought up Mr Hinkley

—26 I mowd some I raked up what I mowd yesterday & to day & got in one load of the hay that was left out on Saturday

—27th I went over & got Niah Hinkley very early & found him in bed. Mr Dyer came while we were at breakfast. We mowd the stubble ground at the corner & also a piece of new ground where the Sandborn wheat grew

Webster Thursday July 28th 1848

Very dull this fore noon Mr Dyer went home to the funeral S Rands daughter who died very sudden, Niah & I spread out the hay put up last Saturday & got it in in the afternoon. I was considerable unwell, with distress in my stomach from eating green cheese this forenoon took some pills at night

—29th Tolerable hay day Dyer & Niah H. mowed some, & spread it out & spread the new ground hay mowd day before yesterday, afternoon raked it all up nearly five tons, I was able to hold the horse rake.

—Sun 30th Very pleasant A. Davis & wife down & I eat a hearty supper that distressd me very much.

—31st Quite unwell in fore noon, we hauld in four load of clover hay & came on to rain before we got in the last load, I very soar & distressed across my bowels, quite an inflamation on my bowels I put on a blister-plaster after dinner powerful rain this afternoon

—August 1st Not much sun in fore noon, but sun enough in afternoon to make the so[?]s to be fit to rake, not able to do anything today, on account of the blister The inflammation abated

—2d Tolerable hay day, able to be our & spread some hay

—3d I am quite smart[1] do not mow any. Mr Dyer, Hinkley & Coursen mow'd

4th Niah went home & R Dyer came over [continued on next page]

---

1 An obsolete use of "smart" meaning "in pain," probably from the blister-plaster TJ applied to his abdomen on the 31st. Whatever he used was clearly potent to have caused this much reaction. Any benefit that blistering conferred would only have been as a counter-irritant. Blister-plasters were used for centuries. They came in various strengths and often included Spanish fly (the beetle *Cantharis vesicatoria* and related insects; a vesicant, cantharidin, is the active agent.) Plasters also might contain pepper, mustard seed ("mustard plasters" were used well into the 20th century), etc. (Thacher, James; *The American New Dispensatory*, Boston 1810)

and we finish'd mowing with the exception of a piece sold to S. Coursen in S.E. corner of the field & the piece by the old house to B. Dyer, some swamp hay raked & out

5th Rainy I am now quite well, powerful shower in afternoon, we sold a firkin of butter to a Mr. Scribner of Lewiston for 15 cents per lb

Sun 6th Quite fair—I spread out hay & got it in

&th I pitched over manure in the yard quite warm B. Dyer mowd his grass

—8th I mowd oats in the old pasture piece in the fore noon B. Dyer help'd me, afternoon I help'd him load his hay & hoed some in the corn by the hard sweet apples, warm

—9th I hoe'd some raked a part of the oats

—10th I mowed some oats in the pasture piece by the springs & got in the oats on the old pasture & ground, very fine & drying

—11th I hoed some & got in more oats

—12th I went to mill early & mowd oats at the lower end of the wheat west of the springs in the fore noon & hoed corn in afternoon, very warm & fine this week

—Sun 13th Foggy this morning but clear & pleasant in the middle of the day we went over to N. J's in afternoon, foggy at night

'4th I went down to Colbys early to get the horse shod I hoed in the garden, piched off oat, pull'd peas &c.

Webster Tuesday August 15th 1848

James Coursen helped me hoe corn & get in one load of oats very warm
—16th J.C. helpd me hoe again
—17th I reap some wheat in the morning & hoed corn the remainder
of the day or until between 8 & 4 oclock P.M. when we had a very
heavy shower. E. Jordan 2d reap some wheat for me in the afternoon
—18th Dull Mr. Courssen dug some potatoes in the morning (& a part
of those were rotten) & I went to mill quite rainy before noon, & very
rainy in afternoon we shelled corn &c.
19th Mr. C. & E. J. 2d helpd me reap wheat in fore noon, & part of the
afternoon until prevented by rain, quite rainy till night
—Sund. 20th We went to meeting, cold raw N.E. wind with heavy
clouds & appearance of rain in fore noon, but more settled in afternoon, my Cousin wife of Apollas Mirllen of Green was buried yesterday & died on the 17th
—21st E Jordan 2d help'd me tie up the wheat & mow on oats &
wheat, cloudy in afternoon with wind N.E.
—22d James Coursen helpd me, he dug some potatoes in fore noon &
turned up wheat & oat & picked out thistles afternoon we raked up
oats & got them in & raked a part of the wheat
—23d We got in the wheat & put the mowd all on the floor, took off
one rack & put it up put on short body & set the cart down in pasture
potatoe piece. Mr Coursen dug some potatoes above the barn & I went
to mill

I & J. Coursen dug potatoes a small yield but fair potatoes & scarcely any rotten, although it is a universal complaint

—25th I set up some wheat, sorted potatoes & pulld peas very cold night for the season & frost in some places

26th I dug some potatoes in fore noon down from the first gate a kind I had of J[?[D. Wentworth which he said last spring had not rotten, but I found them to be rotting, afternoon I carried peas out of potatoes, threshed out some we had in the barn & killd a lamb &c.

—Sun 27th Very fine pleasant day. Quite a general time of health for the season. A young Perie [?[is quite sick at Joshua Jordans

—28th I went to Freeport & got eight bushels plaster, sowd some after I got home, got in some peas, had some rain

—29th sowd plaster in fore noon, Ezekiel Jones came down, & we dug potatoes in afternoon, handsome & no rot—S. Corsen had the oxen to haul his house & run it off Sennets bridge [?[

—30th We finshd the small piece of potatoes, dressed & plowed this spring

—31st James Coursen helpd us dig the remainder of the potatoes in the pasture, very warm & pleasant J. Gould & wife upon a visit

—Sept 1st James Coursen helpd me haul manure in fore noon, rainy in afternoon. Ezekiel helpd me three days

2d I threshed peas in fore noon & got the threshing machine in P.M. & got wet coming home.

Webster Sunday Sept 3d 1848

Some showers in fore noon I did not go to meeting but carried Elizabeth over to Litchfield Corner to school to work her board at S. Bakers

—4th Niah H. came & we set up the machine & threshed the mowd wheat

—5th threshed the remainder being reap in fore noon & winnowd in afternoon 21 bushels in all

—6th & 7th Threshed oats did not finish Niah had the horse to go to Bath

—8gh I went up to Wentworth Jordans to se[e] him in relation to his consenting to stand as a candidate for nomination for Representative, pulld beans in afternoon, quite pleasant

—9gh I pulld beans & went to a caucus to nominate a candidate for Representative first balloting Wentworth Jordan had 30 votes Jesse Davis 25 & Melvin Henderson 20 next balloting W. Jordan had 54 votes & one for someone else J. Davis & M. Henderson declined standing as candidates

—Sun 190th Very fine I wrote a letter to Elizabeth

—11th I killd a pig in fore noon, having recently become lame & went to annual election in afternoon, whig ticket for Governor 121 & Dem 58 W. Jordan elected Representative, fine & pleasant day & first of the evening but rains by ten oclock, smart rain in the morning I finished threshing oats in fore noon. Eld. Stetson & Cousin Sara S. & Lydia S. took dinner with us I went down to Factory ville & carried Eld S. down & I went up to J. B Js and got winnowing machine, Cool N. W. wind

S. Coursen helpd me pull beans in fore noon & cut up corn in afternoon some frost last night & a cold N. W. wind to day

—14th Hard frost in low land, not so as to kill our corn—winno'd oats in fore, & finishd up in afternoon & hauld in beans & shockd corn came on to rain just as night [fell]

—15th Quite rainy in the morning, prepared the beans for drying in the barn, pitched up oat straw &c. in the forenoon S. Coursen helpd me yesterday & to-day by the month, the three last days of each week for a month. I and Mary Ann went up to B. Dyers S. Coursen cut stalks & I cut some after I got home some dashes of rain

—16th Cut stalks &c. cool

—Sun 17th We went to meeting serm. By Eld Stephens We went up to Mr. Robinsons. John & wife from St. Albans being up, some frost again last night but corn is not injured any yet

—18th A very cold N.E. rain storm I shelld corn, & went to mill in afternoon

—19th Pleasant I sowd some plaster, mended fence & yoked rams[1] &c. in fore noon & dug some potatoes in afternoon

—20th I sorted potatoes & picked over some in the cellar (rotting by the way) a part of the fore noon John Robinson & wife here I went to Littleriver in afternoon

---

1 "yoked" in this context would be to apply a wooden device or frame around the neck of the animals to prevent them from escaping through a fence.

Webster Thursday Sept 21st 1848

We dug potatoes S. Coursen & Ezekiel Jones helping, quite pleasant

—22d We dug potatoes in fore noon & rai[ni]ng in afternoon I picked over potatoes in the cellar

—23d We dug potatoes & finished soon after dinner & cut up corn after, cold and windy

Sun. wrth Clear but cool & windy

—24th I shock corn in fore noon & picked seed corn & help'd N. J. shingle on his house in afternoon

—25th I helpd N. J. shingle again

—27th I went over to J. Halls to se a pair of oxen & over to Henry Garcelons to get him to put a window in the kitchen

—28 We haul school wood I got in some corn in afternoon I went over to Crowleys to see a pair of oxen in evening

20th I went over to Crowleys again & bought a pair of oxen in the morning, rainy the remainder of the day we husked corn

—3d We sorted corn in the morning & went over in the pasture to prepare a road to haul stone & hauld stone in afternoon, I went down & shaved Jesse Davis at noon who is quite sick with rheumatism & I sat up with him at night.

Sun Oct 1st Heard that Wm Davis wife at Littleriver vill, was dead & also that Dea. David Pettingill died today

—2d Riny

—3d Very rainy we went to the funeral of Dea. David Pettingill

—4th rainy again, I shaved J Davis at noon

Webster Thursday Oct. 5th 1848

I wheeled[1] some for pigs & gathered apples &c. I went up to A Davis to see a pair of oxen of Wm Crowleys & changed with him & went up to Mr Stanfords & got myself a pair of boots

—6th I gathered apples in for noon quite pleasant & hauld in corn in afternoon

7th We husked all day

—Sun 8th We went down to Niah H.. & brought David Frost home with us to repair the kitchen cold & windy

—9th I helpd Mr Frost on the kitchen about all day & carried him home at night & went to Little river & got a cask of lime & up to Hollands & got hair[2], full moon & pleasant

—10th Some appearance of rain & so we got in corn but did not rain & we husked corn

—11th Lucy Ann & Katherin W[entworth?] had our horse to go over to Litchfield & I went to mill with oxen in fore noon & & got a load of sand in afternoon & put on lathing in kitchen in evening

—12th We slacked lime in the nmoring & & I went up to see if John Pettengill could plaster the kitchen he agreed to come to morrow I sorted corn a part of the afternoon & took off old plastering in eveing, a bad job

13th J. Pettingill plastered & I helpd,

14th Sorted corn in fore noon & got in the last in afternoon

---

1 "Wheeled" may refer to the use of a wheelbarrow for moving material; possibly fodder or manure. At other times, however, TJ uses the term to mean riding or transporting items in a wheeled conveyance.

2. TJ is preparing to plaster his kitchen. He will do this by (1) removing old plaster (2) nailing horizontal thin lathes to the wall or ceiling at intervals to hold the new plaster (3) slaking the lime, adding fine sand and hair to make the actual plaster (the hair acts to bind the plaster and hold it in place after it is applied), and (4) applying the plaster.

Webster Sun. Oct. 15th 1848

I & Ann went to meeting Jesse Davis is some better

15th I set the kitchen window glass & painted closet bedrooms &c

—7th I went to Little river & got jappan[1] & painted kitchen floor in afternoon

—18 I was at D. J. Jones having waggon repair'd & Reuben Dyer told me that his mother was not as well a[s] usual husk'd in evening

—19th Finshd husking some rainy

20th Finish'd sorting corn, put up buts, & cleared out tyup

—21 We went over to haul stone & S. Coursen left to work on his house, I hauld stone in fore noon & painted floors in afternoon

—Sun. 22d I went up to B. Dyers (& Mary Ann went to meeting). Mrs Dyer very low & feeble

—23d I went to Bath sold potatoes for 67 cents, oats for 34 cents & butter for one shilling

—24th We hauld stone in fore noon & hauld manure in afternoon, very pleasant Niah H. & wife up here

—25th Hauld manure, very fine

—26gh Finish'd hauling manure in fore noon & got some carrots & afternoon killd a pig, we went up to see Mrs Dyer who is very low

—27th I started for Bath but sold at Topsham 3/6 for potatoes, 34cts for oats & 7cents for the pig weighing 165, got home & dug carrots in afternoon

----

1 "Japan" was a hard, shiny, black varnish that originally came from Japan. Japan was also used on metal surfaces in place of tinning.

I dug carrots, parsnips &c. wheeled manure I got chaff straw &c. out in the yard. George Jordan came here, the first time since he quit work last year & we went over to Mr Dyers & stayed all night & Mary Ann sat up with Mrs Dyer a part of the night & Hannah Davis the other part. Mrs Dyer is very low & in great distress part of the night, latter part. Some rain in afternoon=of Sunday I did not got meeting

=30th Wm Robinson help'd me break up out east of the house, very warm, being foggy & some mist

=31st I help'd Mr. Robinson's plow, clear & pleasant in fore noon, & foggy in afternoon & misty in evening I did intend to go over & see how Mrs Dyer was but did not get started

=Nov 1st I got up early & went up to Mr Dyers & when I got there found that Mrs Dyer Died last night about eleven oclock I help'd Mr. Robinsons plow in fore noon & went to the funeral of Mr[s] Dyer in afternoon, Mr French preached clear & cool

=3dd I hauld stone all day clear & cool

=4th Hauld stone in fore noon & layed wall in afternoon raw & cloudy

Webster Sun. Nov 5th 1848

At home all day, some rain last night & rainy all day, at night wind S.E. & quite fresh; I heard that Mrs Cushing died last night, wife of John Cushing, has been sick for some time past

I sold a pair of wheels to S & Wm Robinson yesterday for a new sleigh & five dollars in cash

=6th Layed wall quite moderate

=7th We layed wall quite moderate

=7th We layed wall in fore noon & went to Presidential election in afternoon[1]; very pleasant in fore noon & quite a snow squall in afternoon

=8th Very cold in the morning but more pleasant tghrought the day; finishd laying bottoms

—9th Snowing in the morning early, but has the appearance of being moderate; quite a snow again in forenoon, plowed all day in field & pasture; squally & cold at night

=10th Very cold & the ground froze hard this morning & continues cold & windy all day—Hauld away the fence on the W. Side of the last piece plowd in the pasture, dug & hauld stone up to the wall off a piece I intend to plow

=11th I jobd round banked up house; put new back in portch fireplace &c & set pump for N.J. in evening

=Sun 12th We went to meeting serm by Eld Stephens, raw cold & N.E. wind I went up to B. Dyers & got Mary to make dresses

---

1 The preseidential candidates in this election were Zachary Taylor (1784-1850) for the Whigs, Lewis Cass of Michigan (1782-1866) for the Democrats, and the anti-slavery (Free Soil) candidate, former president Martin Van Buren (1782-1862) of New York. Taylor won the three-way election and took office in 1849. He died the following year and was succeeded by his Vice-president, Millard Fillmore (1800-1874).

Webster Monday Nov. 13th 1848

We killd two pigs weighing 266 lbs and 250 lbs, tolerable pleasant& I cut them up in evening

=14th I salted meat &c.

=15th I canted[1] over stumps in the pasture & ground an axe, quite pleasant

=16th Annual Thanksgiving. We went over to J. Goulds or nearly there & met them on their way to Joel Hinkleys to thanksgiving & so I turned & went to John Goulds & spent the day very pleasant and fine wheeling

=17th some rain early I went to Mr Robinsons & agreed with them to help me plow in the pasture=& we plowed all day being quite pleasant, some frost

=18th I hewd some sills for a well platform, cool & frosty at night

Sun. 19th Very fine, not any of us to meeting to day Anah Davis & Drusilla D. came down yesterday ground apples in evening

—20th I put up a cheese & got two & a quarter barrels cider, cold driving snow storm in fore noon & milder & no storm in afternoon

—21st I went down early & got the cider quite cool cleard out the shop & cut out some shoes &c. in after noon

—22d I made Ann a pair of thick shoes. more moderate

—23d I got oxen shod at Colbys, dull

24th I made Rowena a pair of thick shoes & a last

---

1 There are many meanings of the verb "cant;" The most likely here is "turned over."

Smart rain last night & foggy & misty this morning I went over to Litchfield after Elizabeth, found her hale & hearty, having attended school 12 weeks—clear & pleasant in afternoon, the mud quite deep & hard wheeling—my eyes has been uncommon sore for a week past, but some better having washd them in black alder tea   —Sun 26th Not at meeting dull again

27th I went over to Mr Sawyers & L. Small at the request of Jesse Davis as chairman with B. Donnell to run some division lines between land of Sawyer & Small having a dispute about the line between them, did not get through

—28th We went again & finish runing [lines]—more pleasant than yesterday

—29th I went to mill early & got ready a & started for Bath in fore noon & broke the foreward waggon ax before I got to Topsham, sold my load in Brunswick & retd home. I receivd $3.75 for a barrel of cider 35 cents a bushel for oats, 5 cts for potatoes & 7 cts a lb for chickens, moderate & thawed considerable

—30th I helpd put paper on a bedroom & partly put down a platform to the well, quite mild.

Dec. 1st I hauld a hemlock log to the mill in the morning & finishd the platform [continued on next page]

& went to the mill & got plank for the log hauled this morning, quite pleasant

—2d I hauld one load of manure into the garden & hauld five load of dirt out of the yard into the garden in fore noon, came onto rain about noon with smart S.E. wind & increased to a gale at nignt—I got out straw into the yard

—3d Clear & cooler

—4th Very pleaasant & moderate after the morning. S. Coursen helpd me haul dirt into the field. Mary ann quite sick today

—5th I hauld dirt in the fore noon, snowd some & I went to Little River in afternoon. I brok down our waggon & got to Mrs Robinsons. Thawy & mudy, snowd some in evening

—6th I got waggon home & got the ready to thresh in fore noon , snow quite smart—afternooon I thresh'd beans, snowd again, enough for some sleighing

—7th I winnowd beans, I went over to N. Jordan's after Mary Dyer, she was not done there & did not come, quite stormy of hail & sleet

8th, I went up to Mr Stanfords & got a sheep & got a new sleigh of Mr. Robinson's, warm & hazy

—9th I made Milisse a pair of shoes, clear & pleasant

Sun. 10th I carried Mary Dyer home, more hail & sleet today

Webster Monday Dec. 11th 1848

I fitted ox bows & prepard wood sled & hauld some stumps in afternoon, very pleasant

—12th I put up some plank in front of the shed to prevent the cattle from going in, we had two lambs come last night, I made a pair of fills for W. Jordan, dull again today, frose some last night & pretty fair sleighing today

14th & 1r I hauld stumps, the snow is very soft & ground not froze & treads up very much

—15th I repair'd wood sled &c. very soft & foggy & some rain, clears off at night & some cooler

—16th I carried pig to S. D. Wentworths & got horse shod in fore noon & went down to J. Goulds in afternoon came home in evening some hail & sleet

Sun. 17th Very warm & pleasant & clear the most of the day but some rain early this morning—so warm that frogs are out at the spring.

18th E Jordan 2d helpd me plow & haul dirt into the field & make a water course across the ditch, clear & pleasant

—19th S Coursen helpd me haul dirt again across the ditch, very pleasant & frose but little last night, the ground trod up very much

—20th I cut a maple tree & hauld a cut to the mill & got it split for yokes having split one yesterday

Webster Thursday Dec. 21ist 1848

I made a yoke for the four year old oxen & boiled the ends in the evening, cooler

—22d very cold & thick in forenoon I hauld stumps out of the field— & snowd in afternoon some

—23d. I went down to D. I. Jones & got the horse shod & went up to A Davis in evening quite cool, Mary Ann was very sick on our way home & had a very sick night, in great pain

—24th I sent for the Dr. & he came & pronounced her complaint, the cholic & gave physic, it did not opperate & she had but little relief[1]

—25th the Dr came & gave more physic & it opperated & gave some relief but was very sick in the forenoon, I killed a beef heifer in the fore noon, & more moderate, afternoon S. Coursen & P. Dyer helpd me build some stump fence, rainy in afternoon & evening

—26th we built stump fence[2] verry cold & windy

—27th we built stump fence again, very cold in fore noon but calm & more moderate in afternoon, & began to snow before night very fine & dry & snowd some in evening

—28th We had in the morning a great lot of snow & drifted some. I broke out the road in fore noon 2 hours with two pair of oxen

---

1 Mary Ann's "cholic" may well have been a symptom of gall-bladder disease.

2 A "stump fence" made use of the lined-up twisted roots of stumps after they were extracted from the ground.

Webster Thursday Dec. 28th 1848

I went to mill in afternoon & got a chain mended

—29th I broke into the woods in forenoon, The swamp not froze & the snow was 18 inches deep or nearly so—afternoon S. Coursen helpd me haul stumps thick & some snowy

—30th I hauld stumps till one o clock in a thick snow storm & hauld the largest & last, afternoon, sawd some logs & got in some yoke pieces, ground an ax &c.

Sun. 31st. Broke roads two hours self & two pair of oxen, the wind blew smart & the snow flew merrily

—January 1st 1849 I broke out roads one & half hour in fore noon & at work on a yoke for R. Dyer after

—2d Severe cold & windy John Gould Jrn. & wife came here I done something on Reuben's yoke

—4th Brokeout roads three hours self & four oxen, the roads drifted bad, the third was very blustering & the roads not broke out; I done but little except take care of the cattle

—5th I made a yoke for our old oxen Amah Davis came down on a visit & carried Ezekiel home he having boarded here & attended our school

—6th I went to Topsham & Brunswick carried butter & oats, got 40 cts for oats & one shilling for butter [continued on next page]

& on my way home I saw a two horse team in the river & three men present. I heard they got one horse out & lost the other, very poor sleighing

Sun. 7th I went over to N. Jordan & got Cousin Abigail lately from Portland & got home late & did not go to meeting a Christmas celebration at the meeting house this evening adjourned from Christmas eve, cold but bright moon shine

—8th Verey cold indeeed I went up to S. Coursens after an augur to bore staple holes in an ox yoke & went into the woods

—9th I went into the woods & hauld out some logs

—10th I went up to Jason Rands lot & cut & hauld home a large oak but for cart felloes[1], quite cool, S. Robinson & wife here in evening on visit

—11th I was taken with a diziness in my head similar to last fall, went into the woods & hauld out some hemlock logs

—12 I got one load of wood, the same trouble in head daily

—13th I went up to lewston falls to see Doc. Garcelon & to see the engine, cars, rairoad, bridge &c. Amos Davis went up with me the sleighing was fair & weather moderate

---

1 "felloes" are the curved pieces of wood that make up the outer part of a wheel .

Webster Sat Jan. 13th 1849

I spoke of going to see Dr. Garcelon. I went up to se[e] him in relation to a diziness in my head; about the same as last year[1] The Doc. though[t] that the complaint might arise from a fowl state of the stomach or by taking too much animal food & gave me a powder to take at night & an emetic to take tomorrow morning & physic to take in two hours after the operation of the emetic & then drops to take at bed time, I then went to the Depot engine house & out on the rail road bridge & back to Depot again, but the cars had arrived before we got back, but saw passengers leaving the Depot by the gross, the engine, cars, track &c. to one that never beheld the like cannot fail to appear among the wonders of the world, I then came down & took supper at A. Davis' & then home, some rain in evening, took the Doc.s powder at going to bed which opperated as physic, in the night

—Sun 14th I took the emetic & after that had opperation I took the physick which opperated & I had by this time thorough scouring

—15th I was about & took care of the cattle but no improvement of my health

---

1 TJ does not note whether his"diziness" is light-headedness or true vertigo, I suspect the latter, probably from Meniere's disease (labyrinthitis) as previously noted.

Webster Tues. Jan 16th 1849

The snow blew yesterday finely but not very cold, had a fall of light snow 2, or 3 in on the afternoon of 15th to day took care of the cattle & shod one side of the bob sled in afternoon

—17th I went into the woods in the fore noon & broke into the western part, the swamp not frozen—Nathan B. Jordan from new Portland here in afternoon. I carried Ann up to A Davis at night, rather pleasnt through the day but high wind at nigh[t], my head is little or none better, mysterious I think.

—18th I went into the woods in afternoon twice very cold & windy & extremely cold at night

—19th I carried children to school & went up to Mrs Robinsons & brought down Samls wife to cut me out a sack coat, very extreme cold last night & this morning. I think the coldest we have had this winter. I had enough to do to keep a fire & tend the cattle

—20th I carried a hide over to Capt. Asa Garcelons to be tanned, went into J. Harris to get a model[1] of a cheese press, I went into the woods & got some wood in afternoon

—Sun 21st very well in my head to day. J Gould & wife up here, tolerable pleasant

---

1 "model" is an obsolete term for a description of something, in this case a cheese press.

Webster Monday Jan 22d 1849

I went up to Sabattas ville to mill in fore noon & we went over to N Js in evening on a visit quite cool

—23d I went up to S. Coursens he promised to help me chop wood tomorrow, having promisd to help me today & failed me, I then went down to H. Hollands & then up to B. Dyers & engaged D. Carville to come & chop me some cord wood, at .42 cents per cord more moderate than yesterday

—24th S Coursen & I went into the woods, carried team & brought out a load of wood at noon. I hauld in afternoon & S.C. chopd, quite moderate & snow getting soft at night & rains some in evening

—26th Rains quite smartly in he morning. S.C. & I sawed some hemlock logs in fore noon, some rain just before noon & very foggy, afternoon we went into the woods & choped wood E. Jordan 2d helpd us, the wood is fine order for choping, Jesse Davis' wife made us a visit in evening, clear & cooler

—27th Chopd wood in for noon & S. C. in afternoon, I was detained by Timothy Jordan & wife being at our house

—Sun. 28th I was at home all day,, the fits of diziness in my head continue about as formerly, notwithstanding I conform to Dr. Gs directions.

Webster Monday Jan 29th 1849

I hauld wood, S. Coursen agreed to help me, but did not appear

—30th I hauld wood again & D. Carville came to chop some wood by the cord

—31st I hauld wood again & Carvill choped cord wood quite cool

—Feb 1st I hauld two load of wood in fore noon, a smart snow storm the most of the day

—2d I hauld out five load of cord wood

—3d I hauld two load in fore noon, we had a smart snow squall in the morning, so as to prevent us from going to Harpswell [?] & blowed & the snow drifted all the afternoon

—Sun. 4th Broke out road two & half hours self & one pair of oxen, Enoch Hinkley came up from Bath we had a Lecture at our school house in the eventing by D. T. Stevens.

—5th I hauld four load of cord wood after putting iron on wood sled runner cold & cloudy

—6th I hauld five load C. Hinkley went up to mill for me

—7th I hauld four load

—8th I hauld out some poles to pile wood on in fore noon & hauld two load of wood in afternoon. Lavina Marr at our house last night & Abigail Jordan Has made me a large jacket & vest this week, carried her over to N.Js. raw S. West wind & some snow. D. Carvill Ann & Elisabeth went up to B. Dyers in evening

Webster Fri. Feb 9th 1848

S. Carvill was sick & did not chop & I hauld four load of wood in fore noon & had a powerful snow squall & did not haul wood in afternoon, the snow drifted consideraable

10th—I shoveled snow on the road one hour in fore noon, & broke roads one hour in afternoon self & one pair of oxen—very cold indeed in forenoon

—Suu 11th Another snow storm & windy

—12th Very severe cold. A blue cloudy day. N.B. Jordan came home with grass seed. D Carvill could not chop being too cold

13th I bought one bushel of herds grass seed & 25 lb of clover seed of N.B. Jordan & broke out road one & half hour self & oxen—D Carvill commenced on a well by the yard

—14th I hauld wood & D. Carville chop'd

—15th I hauld wood again & D. Carvill finshd chopping very cold all the time

—16th I hauld two load of wood in fore noon & all—I chopd some ash wood at the door in afternoon

—17th A Davis & wife J. Pettingill & wife made us a visit & Rev. D. T. Stephens came 7 stopd with [us]. Clear & cold

—Sun. 18th Grey & cold we went to meeting, a very cold day

—19th D. Carvill commenced on the well again & got down to ledge early I went to Little River, very cold & went over to S. Cushman & bought cast steel for drills

Webster Tues. Feb 20th 1849

I got drills made at Colbys & blowd some in the well[1] we had very good luck in several charges, very cold & freezing last night, people complain of frosty cellars more this winter than for any winter for many years

—21, 22, 23d & 24th We blowd daily in the well & made some progress

—Sun 25th Some snow to day & Albert is quite sick with a cold

—20th I went down to Jones & got drills sharpened & to Factory & got powder of John Tebbets & prosecuted the blowing business in the well

—28th I was not able to do much S. Robinson helpd D. Carvill in the well afternoon—& Wentworth Jordan & wife down here on a visit & I whet a wood saw for him

—2d Reuben Dyer helpd again, & I done but little

—3d Reuben Helpd in fore noon & I help some in afternoon

Sun 4th We went to meeting cool & very clear

5th At work in the well made very slow progress

6th S. C. was sick & I got cart fellowe stuff sawd at the mill

—7th We blowd some in fore noon

---

1 TJ is digging a new well. He began work on February 19th and hit a rock ledge almost immediately. He is now drilling holes and placing black powder charges to break up the rock.

Webster Wednesday, March 7th 1845

I went up to mill in afternoon & up to Greene to see Mace Lane about blowing in the well, he thought that we had pursued about the same course that he should, but, I am almost discouraged, some snow today the first of any amount for sometime

—8th Cold & windy, we made some progress in the well

—9th Cold & windy again, but pleasant sun. I sent to Lewiston by John Bryent to get another fifty feet of fuse, we used the last of the first fifty feet to day

—10th Cold & blustering the snow blows smartly at work in the well

—Sun. 11th We went over on the ridge to Niah H's having not seen him since he returned from Virginia when we got there they told us that Mr. S. Hinkley fell on the floor at home & broke his thigh yesterday morning, we went up to see him, he was tolerable comfortable, quite cold & windy— we upset the sleigh on our way home

—12th I went to Littleriver ville bought a keg of powder of J. Gerrish & ten & half lb steel of J. Tebbets. Horace Dwelley came to work in the well with Daniel C. rather pleasant

—13th I went to Freeport & haauld down ten bushels potatoes & got 4 shilling per bushel & hauled home ½ [?] bush. plaster

Webster Tuesday March 13th 1849

Very warm & pleasant & poor sleighing to get home from Freeport

—14th Still at work in the well H. Dwelley still helping

—15th Daniel C. has a lame hand & did no work & went up to Mr. Stanford's & H Dwelley did not work in afternnon, some snow, N. Hinkley & wife up to day

—16th H. D. & I blowd in he well to day, D. Carvill so lame as not to be able to do anything & so went fishing & brought home five pickerel, his hand being very painful at night

17th H. Dwelley & I blowd to day & have conducted[1] to plank up the well, the dirt falls in to much for safety

Sun 18th I walked to meeting, the snow is soft & slumpy

—19th I hauld logs to the mill early to get plank for the well & hauld some more in the day & hauld home plank & went up to Mr. Stanfords & got a pair of boots for D. Carvill

—20th William Stinchfield & N. J. came & helpd me about planking up the well a strong S. wind to day

—21st some rainy. Wm. S. Held me finish the well in the morning & then I went to work on a pair of wheels for him got out spokes &c.

—22d Wm. S. Helpd me set the spokes & then went over to Ns

21d I went to mill & got a cast spoke of Mr. Davis [continued on next page]

---

1 "have conducted" as used here possibly means "decided to….," but the term also means "to engage (someone) to…."

& set two in Wm S. wheels & whet N. J.s saw & at work on the wheels
—24th I workd off the spokes in s[ai]d wheels

—Sun. 25th Some stormy
—26th I went to Town meeting, Samson Colby, Melvin Henderson & John M. Maxwell chosen Selectmen, Assessors & Overseers of poor. Quite rainy
—27th 28th 29th & 30th in fore noon at work on & finish'd Wm. S. wheels I sold the old oxen to John Crowley in afternoon for $40.00 four days of this week has been rainy I went down to see a pump of B.D. Bryents to put on the new well
—31st I hauld home B. D. Brs pump & put it in the well & got it to work well, very pleasant day
—Sun. April 1st I went over to meeting, but had none Mr. Stephens attended the funeral of Maj. Pray I went over to see Mr. Hinkley, found him quite comfortable, very cold & windy
—2d I made R. Dyer a yoke
3d & 4th I repaired the waggon, made new ex[axle] &c quite pleasant
—5tj Anual fast. I sawd out 24 cart felloes a hard days work, dull & some rain
—6th Cold & windy I winnowd some beans, made well spout, painted yokes, cleaned out pig, shelld corn &c.
—7h I & D. Carvill went to Little River, poor waggoning, went to school meeting

Webster Sunday April 8th 1849

At home all day

9th Went to mill & set[?] by Mr. Robinson

10th & 11th D. Carvill helpd me saw up mill logs & fire wood

—13th I went to Topsham & routed by Bowdoinham to engage appletrees of Pribble

14th I hauld from the well very cold & windy

—Sun 15th I went to meeting very cold indeed

—16th I hauld sone out of the yard & put up the fence by the well very uncommon cold

—17th I hauld logs to the mill too cold to top out wall, Daniel chopd up some wood in the woods—Mary-Ann & Rowena went to Harpswell

—18th we topd out wall, tolerable pleasant

—19th A smart snow storm all day I boild cart fellows

—20 & 21 I helpd Mr Robinsons on wheels. Mary Ann got home on the 20th

Sun. 22d at home

—23d I went to Bowdoinham after appletrees, got home & set them out in afternoon Silas Jordan began work by the month for half the time to day, he pile'd up wood

—24th We hauld dirt for appletrees in fore noon & topd out wall in afternoon

—25th Topd out wall & finisd tolerable pleasant

—26th Simon Carvill grafted for me & I trimmed appletrees

—27th I went to Bath, I got five shilling for some potatoes, 4/6 for some, & oats 2/3

—28th We broke up some down in the pasture in fore noon, I got subscription for Society in afternoon

Webster Sunday April 29th 1849

I went over to meeting. Eld Stephens last Sabbath for the last year, rather cool

30th I hauld boards from the mill

—May 1st I hauld dirt from the well & from the road, up on the ledge, cold nights

—2d I harrowd on a last years potatoe piece, south of the hill in the pasture

3d I harrowd on another piece (broke up last fall & this spring) all day, very cold last night,, Mary Ann went down on the ridge, Mr. Hinkley is so as to set up in bed

—4th Some rain this morning, I stuck up some boards & slats & hauld some boards over in the pasture to fence the potatoe ground, afternoon I built pitch-pole fence, after waiting upon Niah & D. Hinkey, full more pleasant this afternoon than any we have yet had

—5th I sowed oats over on the potatoe ground in the pasture picked up stone harrowd & rolled it all & built some board fence on the hill side of this years potatoe ground.. Silas Jordan had horse & waggon to go to Auburn

Sun. 6th Quite pleasant, heard to day that the Cotton factory at Brunswick was burnt one evening last week

7th The above report is not true, it was the woolen Factory & mills &c. we planted potatoes in the pasture (south of the hill) & put up some fence

8 Finishd the potatoes piece & the fence too [continued on next page]

150

& got off some corn buts

—9th We got off the remainder of corn buts & harrow'd & cultivated the ground for wheat. Some rain in afternoon

—10th We harrowd over the ground that we cultivated yesterday & sow'd three bushels wheat & one bushel barley & grass seed & harrowd & rolld it all

—11 We hauld down three load of manure on the grass ground, spread & plowed it on the upper side of the small potatoe piece on what was the old pasture & sowd the potatoe piece & some of broke up to barley & the remainder of sward land to pear, & seeded it all down. This seeding down new ground is a new e[x]piriment

—12th Plow'd the garden & harrowd for potatoes & furrowd it out & I planted some potatoes in the garden & prepared some for beans

Sun 13th Very remarkable pleasant this morning. We went to meeting, serm. J C. Knowlton with some prospect of his preaching with us this season, the wind blows up from S. & E. quite early in fore noon & continues to increase & rains before night, & quite smart in evening

14th Very powerful rain last night & this morning, I did not do much in fore noon—but piled up small stones at the new well in afternoon

—15th I went to mill in the morning & saw Elijah Jones with a pair of three year old steers

Webster Tuesday May 15th 1849

I went down to the mill with a log & shifted our steers with a pair C. Jones had, & they mated first rate[1], William son of Elijah called on me in afternoon but we could not trade. I hauld away some small stones from the well in afternoon

—16th Daniel Hinkley came to help me & we hauld manure above the barn, he spread after suppper & I went down to George Frosts & carried his waggon home that our girls got to come home, the hind ex of [his?] broke & I brought ours home first

—17th Daniel H. helpd me plow above the ban for corn

—18th I finis'd the piece alone with our oxen in fore noon & harrowd some of it with the horse afternoon finishe'd & harrowd some on the broke up ground east of the house

—19th I Harrowd the broke up ground ready for planting, tolerable pleaasant but has been cold & backward[2]

—Sun 20th Not at meeting, J. Pettingill calld & told us he & wife inteded to start for New York to morrow & we conducted to go up to the depo with them & take home his waggon to use until his return

—21st We started & went up to J. Ps & then went up to the depo with them & saw them start in the cars, we then went to see the R.R. Bridge & down to A Davis & took dinner, then home & did something at planting Silas at work & planted some corn in forenoon

---

1 Apparently TJ and C. Jones joined their steers so that four of them could to work together

2 "backward"= "unseasonable."

Webster Tuesday May 22d 1849

Reuben Dyer helpd us plant to day & got along quite well, dull & signs of rain, Pricilla & Lucy Ham up here & stopd all night

—23d We finished planting corn & put out some manure for potaoes—children & all hands[1] sick at night

—24th Planted potatoes very cold indeed, cold N.E. wind

—25th Hauld some manure & plowd & harrowd a small piece in the N.W. corner of the field for potatoes, Mr. John Atwood buried to day who died in 24th inst.

—26th We finshd planting & I went up to O. Carvills to see if I could get the waggon mended & over & settled wih Dr Garcelon I owed him $5.19.

Sun. 27th We went to meeting very fine & pleasant, we went down to Niah's who are all unwell, then home & down to N.Js.

28th I went up to O. Carvills & got waggon ex mended in fore noon & at work in the garden in afternoon

29th At work in the garden &c. in fore noon & went to Little riverville in afernoon after a barrel of molasses but did not get any & got half a barrel mackerel very fine & drying

—39th I went up to W. Jordans & up to mill, & down to A. Jones & got horse shod for D. Carvill to go to New Portland tomorrow hauld some stumps & mended fence & hauld roots up to the door in afternoon

---

1 When I was a child I was told that Thomas Jordan had been a sea captain. The notation "all hands" and his constant attention to the strength and direction of the wind are the only evidence that would suggest that he had gone to sea.

Webster Thurs May 31 1849

I got the remaining water in the cistern out this morning having nearly all leaked out lately, & then went on the highway to work I went after stone for a watercourse & came onto rain & I went two turn & got very wet, noon when I got home, very rainy in afternoon, I chored around

—June first. I went up & helpd with Mr. Robinsons on their wheels in fore noon & a little while in afternoon, & Thomas Atwood came to stop the leak in cistern but could not find any & went home & I washed it clean & found cracks in the corners—the sun came out in afternooon

2d I had the sheep washd by B. Coursen & strung the corn, pitched over some manure withed[1] fence &c. very fine day

—Sun 3d dull some rain in the morning, cloudy & raw wind in afternoon

4, 5, and 6 at work on the road. The afternoon of fourth we had a powerful shower. the ground is very wet.

—7th T. Atwood cemented cistern, I planted beans, very fine & R. Gould up here

—8 I sheared sheep

—9th I plowed turnip & boiled felloes at Mr Robinsons. Silas sick & went to Doctor

---

1 TJ repaired the fence most likely with branches of some type, possibly willow. A "withe" is a branch or twig that can be used for basketry, mending, binding things together, etc.

Webster Sun. June 10th 1849

We went to meeting serm By Rev. M. French

11th I chopd & split wood at the door & split cord wood mended fence &c

—13, 14, 15th I pealed hemlock bark[1] quite warm days & growing eeather

The 12th I built a bridge to the back barn doors

16th I harrowd corn very warm indeed, much warmer than any previous day this season. Mary Ann had a tooth hauld by Cushing
Sun. 17th We went to Lewiston falls to the funeral of the wife Johathan Raynes, warm again

—18th I went to Little river vill, & got a barrrel of molasses in the morning & hoed corn

—19th finishd weeding corn & cultivated some potatoes

20th hoed & cultivated potatoes, very warm weather

—21st hoed all day & extremely warm too

—22 Finisd hoeing on pasture ground. & then piled up bark in fore noon, very warm indeed, afternoon cultivated potatoes in the field & hoed some

—23d Finishd hoeing potatoes, some cooler

Sun 24th I carried Elisabeth down to her school & got horse shod, shelld corn & went to mill

—26th Pealed & piled bark

—27th I got fence rods at Colbys in fore noon & drilld stone posts in afternoon

—28th Mowed some ground the orchard to build fence & got in the grass

—29th I tapd my boots in fore noon & split stakes in afternoon to put round appletrees

30th I hauld logs to mill for rails & haul rails home &c. &c. [continued on next page]

---

1 bark to be used for tanning.

Mary Ann went to Little river ville, & I repaired Cistern pump

—July 1st Sun Niah H and wife up here, no rain since the fourth of June except a little on the night of the 25th & a little more on the 29th very dry indeed & have very drying weather

2d & 3d I had S. Coursen to help me build a fence round the orchard, We heard on the third that Mary Ann's father had broken his leg again & she went over to see him,[1] Gilbert Row began work for one month on the 2d

—4th I, Ann & Rowena went up to Lewiston & looked round well & got home I completed the fence round the orchard—

With this entry, Thomas Jordan's diary ends. The last few pages, including a final page written on his notebook's free endpage, were written without his usual care. He used a much thicker nib and covered only half of the final page. We have no way of knowing whether he continued his journal, or whether this was an effort that extended only over the period that we have transcribed, between Monday, February 17th, 1845 through the national holiday of July 4th 1849 when he and two of the children went to Lewiston and "looked round well."

---

1 Mary Ann's father fell on March 12th and broke his leg (most likely his hip). It probably remained unset and it was almost to be expected that the healing was either imperfect, or incomplete, or probably both.

A CD is available that contains all of Thomas Jordan's diary, electronically scanned in color at 300 dpi, jpeg format.

To order the compact disk, send $10 check or money order to:

Scott Earle, 2440 N. Bogus Basin Rd., Boise, ID 83702.

Paypal transfers to larkspur1@cableone.net are also accepted.

www.ingramcontent.com/pod-product-compliance
Lightning Source LLC
Chambersburg PA
CBHW021159010426
R18062100002B/R180621PG41931CBX00006B/3